ACAI PUREE

PREP: 10 MIN   BLEND: 2 MIN   SERVES: 2

INGREDIENTS

2 cups frozen mixed berries

1 tbsp acai powder

1 banana

½ cup non-dairy milk

1 tbsp unsweetened almond butter

1 tsp pure vanilla extract

DIRECTIONS

1. In blender, combine berries, acai powder, banana, non-dairy milk, almond butter, and vanilla extract.
2. Blend on high until smooth. If needed, add more non-dairy milk to reach desired consistency.
3. Use for Acai Bowls (see page 11) or freeze.

HELPFUL TIPS

When prepping for future recipe use, divide the puree into 2 equal portions and freeze in a small freezer bag. For a sweeter puree, add a few pitted dates or a drizzle of pure maple syrup before blending.

Recipe contains nut by-products.*

Add other sugar-free toppings, such as chia seeds, hemp seeds, or unsweetened coconut flakes to this Acai bowl for added texture and nutrition.

ACAI BOWLS

PREP: 10 MIN   BLEND: 2 MIN   SERVES: 2

INGREDIENTS

2 packs pre-made frozen Acai puree
or one batch of Acai Puree recipe
(see page 9)
½ cup non-dairy milk
½ banana
½ cup strawberries
½ cup blueberries

TOPPINGS

½ banana, sliced
Kiwi, sliced
Strawberries, sliced
Blueberries, fresh
½ cup granola, no added sugar

DIRECTIONS

1. In blender, combine Acai puree, non-dairy milk, ½ banana, strawberries, and blueberries.
2. Blend, until smooth, and add more non-dairy milk until you reach desired consistency.
3. Divide mixture evenly between two bowls.
4. Top each bowl with banana, kiwi, strawberries, blueberries, and granola.

HELPFUL TIPS

Recipe is high in antioxidants, fiber, heart-healthy fats, minerals, and low in sugar.

A smoothie is a milkshake on steroids.

BLUEBERRY OAT SMOOTHIE

PREP: 5 MIN   BLEND: 2 MIN   SERVES: 2

INGREDIENTS

1 cup non-dairy milk

1½ cups frozen wild blueberries

2 frozen bananas

¼ cup unsweetened almond butter

¼ cup gluten-free old-fashioned oats

1½ cups organic baby spinach

1 tbsp flaxseed

3 dates, pitted

DIRECTIONS

1. Add all ingredients to high-powered blender, and blend on high until smooth.
2. Pour smoothie into glasses.
3. Serve immediately, and ENJOY.

HELPFUL TIPS

Be sure to use a high-powered blender or food processor to ensure the chopping and liquifying of the frozen ingredients.

Recipe contains nut by-products.*

Can't make up your mind?
Put them all in a blender.

VERY BERRY SMOOTHIE

PREP: 5 MIN   BLEND: 2 MIN   SERVES: 2

INGREDIENTS

1 cup non-diary milk
½ cup frozen wild blueberries
1 frozen banana
¼ cup unsweetened almond butter
6-7 frozen strawberries
1½ cups organic baby spinach
1 tsp flaxseed
3 dates, pitted

DIRECTIONS

1. Add all ingredients to high-powered blender, and blend on high, until smooth.
2. Pour smoothie into glasses.
3. Serve immediately, and enjoy.

HELPFUL TIPS

Be sure to use a high-powered blender or food processor to ensure the chopping and liquifying of the frozen ingredients.

Recipe contains nut by-products.*

A healthier version of an old favorite.
The chocolate milkshake...with a hint of mint.

CHOCOLATE MINT SMOOTHIE

PREP: 5 MIN   BLEND: 2 MIN   SERVES: 2

INGREDIENTS

1 cup non-dairy milk

1 frozen banana

2 tbsp cacao powder

6 fresh mint leaves (or 3 drops mint extract)

1½ cups organic baby spinach

1 tsp flaxseed

3 dates, pitted

DIRECTIONS

1. Add all ingredients to high-powered blender, and blend on high, until smooth.
2. Pour smoothie into glasses.
3. Serve immediately, and enjoy.

HELPFUL TIPS

Baby spinach has such a subtle taste that you won't even know it's in there. It's like eating a salad without a fork.

This is a variation of an egg recipe that my husband AL learned from his father, who was a Mess Sgt. in WWII. My father-in-law fed 500 G.I.s at a time with this recipe.

SMOKEY SCRAMBLE

PREP: 5 MIN   COOK: 12 MIN   SERVES: 2

INGREDIENTS

1 can (15 oz) Great Northern
beans, drained and rinsed

½ cup JUST Egg egg substitute

2 cups organic baby spinach

2 garlic cloves, minced

3 drops liquid smoke

1 tbsp vegetable broth

Salt and pepper, to taste

1 medium tomato, sliced

DIRECTIONS

1. Heat broth in large skillet over medium-high heat, add garlic, and sauté, about 1-2 minutes.
2. Add beans to skillet, and cook, about 3-4 minutes, stirring occasionally.
3. Pour in JUST Egg, stir gently, and cook, about 2-3 minutes, until it starts to set.
4. Add spinach, and cook about, 2-3 minutes, until wilted.
5. Stir in liquid smoke, and season with salt and pepper.
6. Garnish with tomato, and serve warm.

HELPFUL TIPS

Liquid smoke adds great flavor to meals. A little bit goes a long way.

Whether you're preparing for a busy morning or looking forward to a leisurely breakfast, these Overnight Oats provide a delicious and wholesome start to your day.

OVERNIGHT OATS

PREP: 10 MIN   CHILL TIME: OVERNIGHT   SERVES: 1

INGREDIENTS

¼ cup old-fashioned oats

2 tsp unsweetened almond
butter

2 tsp cinnamon

1 tsp maple syrup

1 banana, sliced

½ cup non-dairy milk

DIRECTIONS

1. Combine all ingredients in mason jar, and shake, until blended.
2. Place in refrigerator overnight.
3. If oats are too thick when ready to eat, add more non-dairy milk.

HELPFUL TIPS

This dish is a perfect Summer breakfast. Overnight Oats offer a convenient and nutritious breakfast option that's ready to enjoy as soon as you wake up.
Recipe contains nut by-products.*

I could eat this for breakfast, lunch, and dinner. When peppers and beans are gently simmered together in a skillet and infused with aromatic garlic and basil, the magic happens. This tasty combo is one of my favorites.

PEPPERS AND BEANS

PREP: 10 MIN   COOK: 15 MIN   SERVES: 4

INGREDIENTS

2 tbsp vegetable broth

½ orange bell pepper, sliced

½ red bell pepper, sliced

½ cup Great Northern beans, canned, drained, and rinsed

½ cup water

Salt and pepper, to taste

Garlic powder, to taste

Fresh basil, chopped

1 cup organic baby spinach

DIRECTIONS

1. Heat frying pan over medium heat, and add broth.
2. Add bell peppers, sauté for 3-4 minutes, and add beans.
3. Pour in water, salt, pepper, and garlic power. Stir well to combine.
4. Cover, and let simmer over medium-low heat, about 8-10 minutes, stirring occasionally.
5. Once cooked, sprinkle with fresh, basil.
6. Serve hot on bed of spinach.

HELPFUL TIPS

Fresh basil adds a refreshing touch, enhancing the overall taste and appeal of this simple yet delicious meal. A great way to start your day.

This plant-based version replaces eggs with tofu to create a flavorful and satisfying alternative to the traditional Italian pepper and egg sandwich.

ITALIAN PEPPER SCRAMBLE

PREP: 10 MIN   COOK: 20 MIN   SERVES: 4

INGREDIENTS

2 large red bell peppers, chopped

1 large Cubanelle pepper,
seeded and chopped

2 medium onions, chopped

¼ cup water

1¼ tsp kosher salt

¼ tsp black pepper

¼ tsp turmeric powder

1 block (14 oz) firm tofu, pressed
and crumbled

4 buns, whole grain or gluten-
free

Fresh parsley or basil, chopped

DIRECTIONS

1. In large pan, sauté pepper and onion with water over medium heat, about 2 minutes. Cover and cook for 8 minutes.
2. Remove lid, and continue to cook, about 2 minutes. Add more water, if necessary, to prevent sticking.
3. Season with salt, pepper, and turmeric.
4. Crumble tofu into pan, and stir well to combine.
5. Cook over medium-low heat, stirring occasionally, about 5-7 minutes.
6. Spoon on buns, and serve with chopped parsley or basil.

HELPFUL TIPS

Sauteed peppers and onions meld perfectly with tofu scramble, creating a savory filling that's packed with flavor. Served on your choice of whole grain buns or loaf bread, it's a wholesome and satisfying meal.

Start your morning with a comforting bowl of warm, hearty oatmeal that will keep you full for hours. Glucose from the fruit toppings will provide you with your morning energy boost.

COOKED OATMEAL

PREP: 5 MIN   COOK: 10 MIN   SERVES: 2

INGREDIENTS

1 cup old-fashioned oats

2 cups water

Pinch of salt

2 tbsp maple syrup, plus more
for drizzling

½ tsp ground cinnamon

¼ cup raisins

¼ cup walnuts, chopped

2 tbsp maple syrup, plus more
for drizzling

Fresh fruit

DIRECTIONS

1. In medium saucepan, bring water to boil, and add oats and salt.
2. Reduce heat to medium-low, and simmer uncovered, stirring occasionally, about 5-7 minutes, or until oats are tender and mixture has thickened to your desired consistency.
3. Remove from heat.
4. Stir in maple syrup, cinnamon, raisins, and walnuts.
5. Serve hot, topped with additional maple syrup and fresh fruit.

HELPFUL TIPS

Try granola for added crunch. This oatmeal can be stored in the refrigerator for a few days. Add a splash of water before reheating.
Recipe contains nuts.*

You Are What You Eat... Choose Wisely.

CHAPTER 2 SNACKS

Perfect breakfast or snack to have on hand. These treasures are wonderful for traveling and quick treats. Can be eaten warm or cold.

BANANA OAT BARS

PREP: 10 MIN   COOK: 30 MIN   MAKES 16 BARS

INGREDIENTS

3 large ripe bananas, mashed

¾ cup unsweetened coconut, shredded

1 cup raisins or dates, chopped (or ½ cup each)

1 cup unsweetened applesauce

2½ cups old-fashioned oats

DIRECTIONS

1. Preheat oven to 350°F.
2. In large bowl, add bananas, coconut, raisins or dates, applesauce, and mix well.
3. Add oats, and stir, until thoroughly combined.
4. Press firmly into 9x9 inch baking pan, using back of spatula.
5. Bake 30 minutes, until top is lightly browned.
6. Remove from oven, and let cool slightly before cutting into bite-sized bars.
7. Refrigerate for up to 4 days.
8. Enjoy cold, or warm them briefly in microwave for a comforting oatmeal bite.

HELPFUL TIPS

For sweeter bars, drizzle honey or maple syrup over each bar before eating. Try warming them in the microwave to restore that fresh feel and flavor.
Recipe contains nut by-products*

Savor the flavor of these naturally sweetened candied nuts. Try them warm from the oven.

CANDIED NUTS

PREP: 10 MIN **COOK: 18 - 25 MIN** **SERVES: 8**

INGREDIENTS

⅓ cup maple syrup

1½ tbsp unsalted vegan butter, melted

1½ tsp kosher salt or sea salt

2 tsp vanilla extract

¾ tsp ground cinnamon

¼ tsp Cayenne pepper

1 cup raw pecan halves

1 cup cashews

1 cup walnuts

1 cup almonds

DIRECTIONS

1. Preheat oven to 350°F.
2. In medium bowl, combine all ingredients, except nuts, and whisk together.
3. Add nuts, and stir to coat evenly.
4. Spread nuts in single layer on baking sheet lined with parchment paper.
5. Bake for 12 minutes, stir every 5 minutes, until nuts are a deep golden color, about 18-25 minutes.
6. Remove from oven, stir and spread evenly across pan.
7. Separate any large clumps while still warm, and serve.

HELPFUL TIPS

Substitute vanilla extract for Bourbon and cinnamon for pumpkin spice, great for the holidays.

Recipe contains nuts and nut by-products.*

Perfect snack for pre and post workouts. A great source of plant protein. Handy to take with you while traveling or running errands when you don't have time to stop.

PROTEIN ENERGY BITES

PREP: 35 MIN   **CHILL TIME: 1 HOUR**   **SERVES: 24**

INGREDIENTS

Dry Ingredients

½ cup dried cranberries or raisins, chopped

½ cup dates, chopped

¼ cup walnuts, finely chopped

1 cup old-fashioned oats

1 cup unsweetened coconut shreds

¼ cup ground flaxseed

¼ cup ground hemp seeds

¼ cup raw pumpkin seeds, crushed

¼ cup chia seeds

1 tbsp unsweetened cocoa powder

Wet Ingredients

1 cup unsweetened almond butter

½ cup pure maple syrup or honey

2 tsp vanilla extract

2-4 tsp water or vanilla extract

DIRECTIONS

1. In large bowl, mix dry ingredients.
2. In small bowl, mix wet ingredients.
3. Combine wet and dry ingredients, and mix by hand.
4. Place in refrigerator for an hour, or until firm.
5. Form into bite-sized balls, about 2 tbsp each.
6. If mixture is too dry, add additional water or vanilla extract. If too wet, add more oats and coconut. The dough should be slightly sticky.
7. Enjoy immediately, or store in an airtight container for up to a week.

HELPFUL TIPS

Optionally, once formed, roll bites in coconut or chopped nuts. As an alternative serving suggestion, press the mixture into a 9x9 pan, and cut into bite-sized squares. Try freezing a batch to use as needed, or just a few at a time.

Recipe contains nuts and nut by-products.*

Kale chips are a delicious crunchy snack alternative. Get your antioxidant protection from a green leafy snack.

KALE CHIPS

PREP: 10 MIN   **COOK: 20 MIN**   **SERVES: 4**

INGREDIENTS

1 bunch fresh kale

Nutritional yeast

Garlic powder

Sea salt

Pepper

Avocado oil spray

DIRECTIONS

1. Preheat oven to 375 F.
2. Rinse kale thoroughly under cold water, pat dry, and remove tough center stem from each leaf.
3. Tear into bite-sized pieces, approximately 1-2 inches.
4. Spread in single layer on baking sheet lined with parchment paper.
5. Lightly spray kale leaves with avocado oil.
6. Season with nutritional yeast, garlic powder, sea salt, and pepper.
7. Bake for 10 minutes.
8. Carefully flip, and bake for an additional 10 minutes, until crispy and lightly browned. Watch closely to prevent burning.
9. Remove from oven, and let cool slightly before serving.

HELPFUL TIPS

Ensure kale is thoroughly dried after rinsing to achieve crispy chips. Kale chips are best enjoyed immediately after baking for optimal crispiness. Try different seasonings, such as smoked paprika or Cayenne pepper for a spicy kick.

These little gems may look and snack like nuts, but they are loaded with protein and have much less fat. A perfect addition to your snack drawer.

ROASTED CHICKPEAS

PREP: 5 MIN   COOK: 30-35 MIN   SERVES: 4

INGREDIENTS

1 can (15 oz) chickpeas, drain
and rinse

1 tbsp chickpea liquid

1 tsp smoked paprika

½ tsp garlic powder

½ tsp ground cumin

¼ tsp Cayenne pepper

½ tsp sea salt

¼ tsp ground black pepper

DIRECTIONS

1. Preheat oven to 400°F.
2. Spread chickpeas on clean kitchen towel or paper towel, and pat dry. The drier the chickpeas, the crispier they will be.
3. In large bowl, add remaining ingredients and combine. Add chickpeas, and ensure they are evenly coated.
4. Spread in single layer on baking sheet lined with parchment paper.
5. Bake for 30-35 minutes, stirring or shaking pan halfway through, until crispy and golden brown.
6. Remove from oven, and let cool. They will continue to crisp as they cool. Once cooled, transfer to serving bowl.

HELPFUL TIPS

Throw a handful in a bag for an easy travel snack. A perfect way to add more protein to your day by tossing on a salad or adding to a soup.

The Power
of Plants

CHAPTER 3 APPETIZERS

This low calorie, high protein dish turned me into a tofu fan. The recipe is rich in flavor, making it a healthy choice for any meal.

TOFU "CHICKEN" STRIPS

PREP: 60 MIN *COOK: 15 MIN* *SERVES: 4*

INGREDIENTS

1 block (14 oz) extra-firm tofu, pressed, cut into ½ inch slices

2 tbsp Liquid Aminos or tamari

1 tbsp nutritional yeast

2 tsp garlic powder

1 tsp onion powder

1 tsp smoked paprika

¼ tsp black pepper

¼ tsp turmeric

3 tbsp vegetable broth or water

DIRECTIONS

1. Preheat oven to 425 F.
2. In small bowl, whisk together all ingredients, except tofu.
3. Add tofu, and coat evenly. Marinate for at least 30 minutes, ideally, overnight in refrigerator.
4. Place tofu in baking dish, and bake for 20 minutes.
5. Flip, and bake an additional 15 minutes.
6. Broil for 2 minutes on each side, until edges begin to crisp and turn golden brown.

HELPFUL TIPS

Tofu can be used in a variety of dishes, from savory to sweet, and can be prepared in many ways, including grilling, stir-frying, blending, or baking, making it a versatile addition to many meals.

Rediscover Cauliflower. Barbeque Bites are a healthy twist on a classic appetizer or snack. Perfect for parties or as a flavorful side dish. It's our #1 appetizer while watching our favorite teams.

CAULIFLOWER BARBECUE BITES

PREP: 15 MIN   *COOK: 25 MIN*   *SERVES: 4*

INGREDIENTS

1 head cauliflower, cut into florets

1 cup barbecue sauce

2 tbsp Liquid Aminos or tamari

1 tbsp maple syrup

1 tsp smoked paprika

½ tsp garlic powder

Salt and pepper, to taste

Fresh parsley or green onions, chopped

DIRECTIONS

1. Preheat oven to 425°F.
2. In large bowl, whisk together all ingredients, except cauliflower, parsley and green onions.
3. Add cauliflower, and mix until well coated. Arrange in single layer on baking sheet lined with parchment paper.
4. Bake for 20-25 minutes, until tender and caramelized around the edges, flipping halfway through.
5. Remove from oven, and let cool slightly.
6. Sprinkle with parsley or green onions.
7. Serve warm.

HELPFUL TIPS

These Cauliflower Barbecue Bites are packed with flavor and nutrients, making them a guilt-free indulgence for any occasion. See my Ranch Dressing recipe (see page 168) for dipping.

Ciabotta Abruzzo, with eggplant as its primary ingredient, provides fiber, vitamins (especially B vitamins), and minerals, like potassium and manganese. It is a cherished staple in many Italian households.

CIABOTTA ABRUZZO

PREP: 15 MIN **COOK: 25-37 MIN** **SERVES: 4**

INGREDIENTS

1 medium eggplant, chopped into 1 inch pieces

1 medium zucchini, chopped into 1 inch pieces

1 large yellow onion, chopped into 1 inch pieces

1 red bell pepper, chopped into 1 inch pieces

½ cup red wine vinegar

2 tbsp monk fruit sweetener or stevia

1 tbsp tomato paste

¼ cup vegetable broth

¼ cup fresh basil, torn

Salt and pepper, to taste

4 Ciabatta

DIRECTIONS

1. In large, non-stick skillet over medium heat, add partial broth and eggplant. Season with salt, cover, and cook, about 10-15 minutes, stirring occasionally, until tender and lightly browned. Transfer to bowl.
2. In skillet, add more broth and zucchini. Season with salt, cover, and cook, about 5-8 minutes, stirring occasionally, until tender. Add to bowl with eggplant.
3. Add more broth to skillet and add onion and bell pepper. Season with salt, cover, and cook, about 7-10 minutes, stirring occasionally, until softened and starts to brown.
4. Stir in red wine vinegar, sweetener, and tomato paste. Continue cooking, about 1-2 minutes, until liquid reduces slightly and becomes syrupy.
5. Add mixture to bowl with eggplant and zucchini, and stir to combine.
6. Just before serving, season with pepper, and stir in basil.
7. Slice Ciabatta, and top with Abruzzo mix.

HELPFUL TIPS

Serve the Ciabotta warm or at room temperature. Abruzzo also pairs well with crusty bread as an appetizer. Eggplant's ability to absorb flavors and its diverse culinary uses make it a versatile ingredient in various dishes, adding both taste and nutrition.

This incredible Deviled Eggz recipe is truly the closest
I've found to this legendary favorite,
and they are potato based.

DEVILED EGGZ

PREP: 45 MIN　　　*COOK: 45 MIN*　　　*SERVES: 6*

INGREDIENTS

15 mini golden potatoes

3½ oz firm tofu, crumbled

¼ cup vegan mayonnaise

1 tsp Dijon mustard

1 tsp apple cider vinegar

1 tsp nutritional yeast

¼ tsp salt

¼ tsp black salt (Kala namak)

2 tbsp non-dairy milk

¼ tsp onion powder

⅛ tsp ground turmeric

⅛ tsp smoked paprika

DIRECTIONS

1. Boil potatoes until fork tender, about 12-20 minutes. Drain and rinse with cool water.
2. Halve cooled potatoes lengthwise, scoop out potato centers, and place in bowl.
3. Add remaining ingredients.
4. Using an electric mixer or food processor, blend, until mostly smooth.
5. Fill each potato half with mixture, using pastry bag or spoon.
6. Sprinkle with paprika, and serve immediately or refrigerate until ready to serve.

HELPFUL TIPS

To save time, these can be made a day in advance and kept in refrigerator, perfect to be taken to a neighborhood BBQ, family gathering, or potluck.

When making an appetizer, your goal is to keep the ingredients as whole and unprocessed as possible, like this Hummus Flatbread.

HUMMUS FLATBREAD

PREP: 15 MIN   *SERVES: 4*

INGREDIENTS

2 containers (8 oz each) red
pepper hummus

4 slices whole grain flatbread

½ cup parsley, chopped

8 green onions, chopped

1½ cups roasted red peppers,
thinly sliced

4 handfuls spinach, torn

2 tomatoes, sliced

Balsamic glaze or Dijon mustard

DIRECTIONS

1. Scoop hummus onto toasted flatbread.
2. Sprinkle with parsley, green onions, and roasted red peppers.
3. Top with spinach and tomatoes.
4. Drizzle with balsamic glaze or Dijon mustard.

HELPFUL TIPS

May substitute flatbread with rice cakes or lettuce leaves. Add any additional toppings of your choice. It's fun to experiment customizing recipes to your taste.

Crisp, hydrating, and incredibly easy to make, these refreshing Cucumber Bites are a delightful appetizer, perfect for sharing with friends and family.

CUCUMBER BITES

PREP: 15 MIN   MAKES: 24 BITES

INGREDIENTS

2 cucumbers, sliced into ½ inch
rounds
Hummus, any flavor
Cherry tomatoes, halved

DIRECTIONS

1. Using small spoon or melon baller, gently scoop out seeds from center of each cucumber round, taking care not to create holes.
2. Fill with dollop of hummus.
3. Top with halved cherry tomato.
4. Serve immediately.

HELPFUL TIPS

To elevate the presentation, peel evenly-spaced stripes on cucumbers before slicing into rounds. For another option, substitute hummus with guacamole or cucumbers with gluten-free crackers.

Dates provide natural sweetness without added sugars. They support digestive health and help regulate blood sugar levels.

STUFFED DATES

PREP: 15 MIN   SERVES: 12

INGREDIENTS

12 Medjool dates, pitted

¼ cup raw almonds, chopped

¼ cup raw cashews, chopped

¼ cup raw walnuts, chopped

¼ cup unsweetened shredded coconut

2 tablespoons almond butter

1 teaspoon vanilla extract

Pinch of sea salt

DIRECTIONS

1. In small bowl, combine nuts, coconut, almond butter, vanilla, and salt. Stir well, until combined.
2. Slice each date lengthwise, and spoon in mixture.
3. Chill, about 10 minutes, and serve.

HELPFUL TIPS

They make a great snack or appetizer for any occasion.
Recipe contains nuts and nut by-products.*

Be Stronger Than Your Excuses

CHAPTER 4 MAIN DISHES

Mashed chickpeas offer a hearty, protein-rich filling that mimics the taste and texture of a traditional deli tuna sandwich. My hubby loves it.

TASTES LIKE TUNA SANDWICH

PREP: 10 MIN   COOK: 5 MIN   SERVES: 4

INGREDIENTS

1 can (15 oz) chickpeas, drained and rinsed

¼ cup vegan mayonnaise

1 tbsp Dijon mustard

1 tbsp lemon juice

1 tbsp nutritional yeast

½ tsp onion powder

½ tsp garlic powder

1 tbsp dulce or seaweed

Salt and pepper, to taste

4 slices bread, whole grain or gluten-free, toasted

Lettuce leaves

1 tomato, sliced

1 cucumber, sliced

DIRECTIONS

1. In medium bowl, add chickpeas, and pat dry with paper towel. Mash, leaving some texture.
2. Add mayonnaise, Dijon mustard, lemon juice, nutritional yeast, onion powder, garlic powder, dulce or seaweed, salt and pepper, and stir well.
3. Assemble sandwich with mixture, lettuce, tomato, and cucumber.
4. Serve immediately.

HELPFUL TIPS

Enjoy this plant-based alternative to a classic sandwich without gluten or dairy. Try it on a toasted whole grain bun loaded up deli style for a real taste treat.

I can't say enough about "easy". They don't get much easier than this one. Remember to always check for zero added sugars in bottles of BBQ sauce.

BBQ BLACK BEAN SANDWICH

PREP: 10 MIN   COOK: 10 MIN   SERVES: 4

INGREDIENTS

½ yellow onion, chopped

2 garlic cloves, minced

1 can (15 oz) black beans, drained and rinsed

½ cup low sugar BBQ sauce

4 burger buns, whole grain or gluten-free

Optional Toppings:

Coleslaw (see page 149)

Pickles

Lettuce

Additional BBQ sauce

DIRECTIONS

1. Heat frying pan over medium-high heat, add splash of water, onion and garlic, and sauté for 5 minutes, until softened and start to brown.
2. Add black beans and BBQ sauce. Cook for 5 minutes, stirring occasionally, until heated through.
3. Scoop bean mixture onto each bun. Add optional toppings, and serve.

HELPFUL TIPS

Satisfying lunch that's both delicious and oil-free. Perfect for those looking to enjoy a plant-based meal with BBQ taste.

This adult and kid-friendly version of a grilled cheese sandwich takes healthy fun food to a new level.

MASHED POTATO QUESADILLA

PREP: 15 MIN   COOK: 15 MIN   SERVES: 2

INGREDIENTS

4 potatoes, peeled and diced
2 scallions, finely chopped
½ cup non-dairy cheese, shredded
4 tbsp non-dairy butter
Salt and pepper, to taste
4 tortillas, whole grain or gluten-free
Salsa
Sour cream, non-dairy

DIRECTIONS

1. Boil or steam potatoes, about 15-20 minutes, until fork tender. Drain, and mash, until smooth. Season with salt and pepper.
2. Stir in scallions and cheese.
3. Evenly spread potato mixture on two tortillas.
4. Place remaining two tortillas on top to form sandwiches.
5. Heat skillet or griddle over medium heat. Spread butter on outside of each tortilla.
6. Place each quesadilla in skillet, and cook, about 3-4 minutes on each side, until crispy and golden brown.
7. Remove from heat, and cut quesadillas into wedges.
8. Serve hot with salsa and non-dairy sour cream.

HELPFUL TIPS

For additional protein, add black beans to mashed potato mixture, and serve with quacamole for extra flavor.

The velvety, cheesy flavor is not just for kids anymore. Always keep whole grain pastas on hand in the pantry. This Mac-N-Cheez can be whipped up in a flash.

MAC-N-CHEEZ

PREP: 10 MIN   COOK: 20 MIN   SERVES: 4

INGREDIENTS

1 box (12 oz) pasta, whole grain or gluten-free, cooked

For Cheez Sauce

⅓ cup raw cashews, soaked in water*

1½ cups butternut squash, cooked

2 cups unsweetened non-dairy milk

¼ cup nutritional yeast

1 tbsp lemon juice

1 tsp garlic powder

1 tsp onion powder

2½ tbsp Dijon mustard

Salt and pepper, to taste

Optional Ingredients

1 cup broccoli, chopped

1cup peas

1 cup baby organic spinach, torn

Fresh parsley or chives, chopped

DIRECTIONS

1. Preheat oven to 350° F.
2. In blender, combine cheez sauce ingredients, and mix, until smooth and creamy.
3. Pour sauce into saucepan, and heat over medium-low heat, stirring frequently, until warmed through and slightly thickened, about 5-7 minutes. Season with salt and pepper.
4. Combine pasta, sauce, broccoli, (peas and/or spinach, if using) in baking dish.
5. Bake uncovered for 20-35 minutes, until golden brown and bubbly.
6. Garnish with fresh parsley or chives, and serve.

HELPFUL TIPS

Soaking cashews for at least two hours or overnight helps to soften, making them easier to blend into a creamy sauce. No need to soak if using a high-powered blender, such as a Vitamix. Adjust consistency of sauce by adding more non-dairy milk.

Recipe contains nuts and nut by-products.*

My first "plant-based" burger was a mushroom. Still #1 twelve years later, with raw onion, ketchup, and mustard.

PORTOBELLO BURGERS

PREP: 25 MIN   COOK: 15 MIN SERVES: 4

INGREDIENTS

4 Portobello mushrooms, scored*
4 tbsp Liquid Aminos or tamari
4 tbsp Worcestershire sauce
2 tbsp garlic, minced
4 burger buns, whole grain or glute-free

*Very lightly score lines, allowing mushroom to easily separate when biting into it.

DIRECTIONS

1. Clean mushrooms, removing stems, and carefully spooning out gills. Gently rinse under cold water and score.
2. In a bowl, mix together remaining ingredients.
3. Place mushrooms in glass container, add marinade, and coat evenly. Marinate for 10 minutes on each side.

Cooking Options

1. To grill: Preheat grill to medium-high heat. Grill mushrooms, about 5-7 minutes on each side, until tender and grill marks appear.
2. To bake: Preheat oven to 375°F. Place mushrooms on baking sheet lined with parchment paper, and bake, about 15 minutes, or until tender.
3. Serve immediately on burger buns.

HELPFUL TIPS

Serve with toppings, such as lettuce, tomato, avocado, or condiments of choice...just like a regular burger. My husband loves it with A-1 sauce.

The flavor of leftovers always seems to improve with age, especially in this dish. The many healthy benefits of these high fiber, low calorie ingredients are a testament to old world Asian cuisine.

ASIAN VEGGIE BOWL

PREP: 15 MIN   COOK: 20 MIN   SERVES: 4

INGREDIENTS

2 tbsp vegetable broth

1 onion, diced

3 cloves garlic, minced

1 red bell pepper, thinly sliced

1 yellow bell pepper, thinly sliced

1 cup broccoli florets

1 cup snap peas, trimmed

1 can (14 oz) coconut milk

2 tbsp Liquid Aminos or tamari

1 tbsp fresh ginger, minced

1 lime, juiced

1 tbsp sriracha sauce, optional, for heat

Salt and pepper, to taste

2 cups rice or rice noodles, cooked

Fresh cilantro or green onions

DIRECTIONS

1. In large skillet or wok, heat broth over medium heat. Add onion and garlic, sauté until onions are translucent, about 3-4 minutes.
2. Add bell peppers, broccoli, and snap peas. Cook for 5-7 minutes, stirring occasionally, until tender.
3. Remove from heat, and let cool to room temperature.
4. In mixing bowl, combine coconut milk, Liquid Aminos or tamari, ginger, lime juice, and sriracha. Stir into a creamy dressing.
5. Pour dressing over vegetables, and toss gently to coat evenly.
6. Cover, and refrigerate for at least 1 hour to chill thoroughly. Salt and pepper.
7. Serve chilled over rice or rice noodles.
8. Garnish with fresh cilantro or green onions, and serve.

HELPFUL TIPS

Substitute cooked rice with cooked cauliflower rice. Garnish with fresh cilantro or green onions for added freshness, and enjoy this chilled, flavorful, whole food, plant-based meal.

Recipe contains nut by-products.*

Customize your wrap and make it a one-of-a-kind. I pile my veggies so high that sometimes the wrap won't close.

HUMMUS WRAPS

PREP: 10 MIN   *SERVES: 4*

INGREDIENTS

4 large tortillas, whole grain or
gluten-free
1 cup red pepper hummus
1 cup organic baby spinach
1 cup carrots, shredded
1 cucumber, thinly sliced
1 red bell pepper, thinly sliced
1 avocado, sliced
¼ cup red onion, thinly sliced
Salt and pepper, to taste

DIRECTIONS

1. Lay tortillas on clean surface.
2. Spread a generous amount of hummus on each tortilla.
3. Layer spinach, carrots, cucumber, pepper, avocado, and onion on each tortilla.
4. Salt and pepper.
5. Fold in each side of tortilla, and roll up tightly.
6. Slice each wrap in half, and serve immediately.

HELPFUL TIPS

Squeeze lemon into hummus for a fresh and tangy flavor.

My family's new go-to burgers. Packed with plant-based protein from black beans, fiber from a variety of vegetables, and gluten-free oats for binding, these burgers are both satisfying and healthy.

BEAN BURGER

PREP: 15 MIN   *COOK: 14 MIN*   *SERVES: 4*

INGREDIENTS

2 cups black beans, cooked and drained

½ cup old-fashioned oats, ground into flour

¼ cup onions, finely chopped

2 cloves garlic, minced

½ cup carrots, finely grated

¼ cup red bell peppers, chopped

¼ cup fresh cilantro or parsley

2 tbsp tomato paste

1 tsp smoked paprika

1 tsp cumin powder

Salt and pepper, to taste

2 tbsp vegetable broth

4 buns, whole wheat or gluten-free

DIRECTIONS

1. In large bowl, mash beans, leaving some whole for texture.
2. Add oats, onions, garlic, carrots, peppers, cilantro, tomato paste, smoked paprika, cumin, salt, and pepper, and mix well.
3. Divide mixture into equal portions, and form into patties. If the mixture is too wet, add more oats.
4. Heat broth in non-stick skillet over medium heat. Cook, about 5-7 minutes on each side, until crispy and heated through.
5. Serve on buns with favorite toppings and condiments.

HELPFUL TIPS

Try mixing equal parts ketchup and vegan mayonnaise with a dollop of mustard for a high end taste experience.

A long-time favorite for adults and kids alike. Great source of beta carotene and powerful antioxidants.

CARROT HOT DOGS

PREP TIME: 15 MIN   COOK TIME: 15 MIN   REST TIME: 15 MIN   SERVES: 6

INGREDIENTS

6 large carrots, peeled

2 cups low-sodium vegetable broth or try making your own (see page 130)

6 hot dog buns, whole grain or gluten-free

For Marinade

¼ cup apple cider vinegar

3 tbsp Liquid Aminos or tamari

1½ tbsp maple syrup

1 tbsp liquid smoke

1 tsp smoked paprika

2 cloves garlic, roughly chopped

¼ tsp ground black pepper

½ tbsp Worcestershire sauce, vegan

DIRECTIONS

1. Trim carrots to same length as buns. Cut thin end off, keeping as much of thicker part as possible. Shave carrots to make them uniform in width. Optionally, round ends to resemble a hot dog.

2. In medium sauce pan, mix all marinade ingredients. Add carrots, and bring to boil over medium-high heat. Reduce heat, and simmer until fork tender, about 12-15 minutes. Cooking time may vary, depending on thickness of carrots. Remove from heat, and let sit for 15 minutes.

3. Place on bun, and add toppings of your choice. Get creative, and have fun.

HELPFUL TIPS

Double or triple this recipe to have leftovers. For a real treat, try grilled. Brush cooked carrots with avocado oil, place on prepared grill, and cook for 3-5 minutes, or until grill marks appear. Flip and grill for another 3-5 minutes. Monitor closely to avoid burning.

Veggies are a delicious fuel source. The days of boiling away your nutrients are gone. Roast 'em baby.

ROASTED VEGGIES

PREP: 15 MIN**COOK: 30 MIN****SERVES: 4-6**

INGREDIENTS

2 large sweet potatoes, peeled
and chopped
2 bell peppers, any color
1 large red onion, chopped
1 large zucchini, chopped
1 small cauliflower, chopped
1 small broccoli, chopped
2 tbsp Liquid Aminos or tamari
1 tbsp balsamic vinegar
1 tsp garlic powder
1 tsp dried thyme
Salt and pepper, to taste
Fresh parsley or cilantro

DIRECTIONS

1. Preheat oven to 425°F.
2. Place vegetables in large bowl.
3. In small bowl, whisk together Liquid Aminos or tamari, balsamic vinegar, garlic powder, dried thyme.
4. Pour mixture over vegetables, and toss well to coat.
5. Spread vegetables evenly in single layer on large baking sheet lined with parchment paper.
6. Roast, about 25-30 minutes, or until tender and slightly caramelized, stirring halfway through.
7. Remove from oven, and let cool slightly. Salt and pepper.
8. Garnish with fresh parsley or cilantro, and serve.

HELPFUL TIPS

This dish can be transformed by adding or swapping spices to your taste. Customize vegetables based on what you have on hand or prefer. Try roasting the veggies separately to allow the flavors to meld together naturally.

Jackfruit is packed with essential vitamins and minerals, including vitamin C, vitamin A, potassium, magnesium, and iron. It mimics the texture of "pulled" BBQ sandwiches well. Top with coleslaw or pickles for extra crunch & flavor.

PULLED JACKFRUIT SANDWICH

PREP: 15 MIN   COOK: 25 MIN   SERVES: 4

INGREDIENTS

2 cans (10 oz each) young green jackfruit in water, drained, rinsed, and shredded

1 small onion, finely chopped

2 cloves garlic, minced

½ cup vegetable broth + 2 tbsp

½ cup BBQ sauce, gluten-free, no added sugar

1 tbsp Liquid Aminos or tamari

1 tbsp maple syrup

1 tsp smoked paprika

½ tsp ground cumin

½ tsp chili powder

Salt and pepper, to taste

4 burger buns, whole grain or gluten-free, toasted

DIRECTIONS

1. Pat dry jackfruit with paper towels.
2. Heat 2 tbsp broth in a large skillet over medium heat. Add onion and sauté until softened, about 3-4 minutes.
3. Add garlic and sauté for another 30 seconds, then add jackfruit.
4. In a small bowl, mix broth, BBQ sauce, Liquid Aminos or tamari, maple syrup, smoked paprika, cumin, and chili powder.
5. Pour the mixture over the jackfruit and stir well to coat.
6. Simmer uncovered for 20-25 minutes, stirring occasionally, until the jackfruit is tender and the sauce has thickened. If the sauce is too thick, add a splash of water or broth.
7. Spread the pulled jackfruit on buns and serve immediately.

HELPFUL TIPS

Customize your sandwich. Try loading it with BBQ sauce, or smothering it in onions if that's your thing. Be different, be daring...remember, these recipes are your guide to new taste sensations, so enjoy them.

Get creative, mix and match, and above all, enjoy this complex carbohydrate. A baked potato fully loaded with plant-based goodies can stand alone as a satisfying meal.

LOADED BAKED POTATO

PREP: 10 MIN   *COOK: 45 - 60 MIN*   *SERVES: 4*

INGREDIENTS

4 large russet potatoes, washed and dried
Plant-Based Toppings:
non-dairy butter, non-dairy sour cream, non-dairy cheese, chopped fresh chives or green onions, steamed broccoli, sautéed spinach, grilled asparagus, roasted cherry tomatoes, black beans, sautéed mushrooms, guacamole, salsa, hummus, roasted red peppers, caramelized onions, plant-based bacon bits, sriracha or hot sauce

DIRECTIONS

1. Preheat oven to 400°F.
2. Pierce potatoes with fork or knife.
3. Place prepared potatoes directly on oven rack or baking sheet lined with parchment paper.
4. Bake, about 45-60 minutes, or until potatoes are tender.
5. Remove from oven, and let cool.
6. Slice each potato lengthwise, and fluff inside with fork.
7. Serve with favorite toppings.

HELPFUL TIPS

A Baked Potato is my quick go-to meal after a long day at the office or one of my "life happens" busy days. Microwave and eat with your favorite toppings. Smile, it's that simple.
Recipe contains nut by-products.*

Healthy fat from peanut butter combined with the natural sugar from honey, create a sandwich that energizes and keeps you satiated, and kids love it too.

PB AND HONEY SANDWICH

PREP: 5 MIN   *SERVES: 1*

INGREDIENTS

2 slices whole grain or gluten-
free bread
2 tbsp natural peanut butter (no
added sugar or oil)
2 tbsp honey
Banana or apple, slices

DIRECTIONS

1. Spread peanut butter on one slice of
   bread, and drizzle honey on top.
2. Add banana or apple.
3. Place second slice of bread on top to
   form a sandwich.
4. Cut in half. Serve immediately.

HELPFUL TIPS

Enjoy it as a nutritious and delicious snack or meal that's sure to please both kids and adults alike. Perfect for travel lunches, picnics, or extra energy boosts for those long hikes.
Recipe contains peanut by-products.*

Enjoy the benefits of beans in your burrito. These amazing complex carbohydrates are loaded with protein, fiber, and vitamins that aid in many chronic conditions. Fill that burrito, be happy.

BEAN BURRITO

PREP: 10 MIN   COOK: 1-2 MIN   SERVES: 4

INGREDIENTS

2 tortillas, whole grain or gluten-free

1 can (15 oz) refried beans, fat free, mashed

½ cup salsa

½ avocado, mashed

½ can (6 oz) black olives, chopped

1 tomato, chopped

¼ cup non-dairy shredded cheddar cheese

2 cups organic baby spinach, chopped

¼ cup yellow onion, finely chopped

DIRECTIONS

1. In medium bowl, mix beans, salsa, and avocado. Warm in microwave, about 30-60 seconds.
2. Place tortilla in microwave for 10 seconds to make pliable.
3. Spoon generous amount of bean mixture in center of each tortilla, and spread evenly.
4. Add black olives, tomato, cheese, spinach, and onion.
5. Roll tortilla into burrito, and serve immediately.

HELPFUL TIPS

Packed with vibrant flavors and nutritious ingredients. Whether enjoyed warm or cold, they make a versatile choice for lunch or dinner, providing a satisfying balance of textures and tastes. Try adding mango salsa for a twist. Also, substitute the wraps with butter lettuce or Romaine lettuce to increase your intake of leafy greens.
Recipe contains nut by-products.*

Ideal as a side dish or hearty main course, this oil-free grilled eggplant promises to satisfy with its robust flavors and wholesome goodness.

GRILLED EGGPLANT

PREP: 10 MIN   COOK: 10 MIN   SERVES: 4

INGREDIENTS

2 medium eggplants, sliced into
½ inch rounds or lengthwise strips

2 tbsp balsamic vinegar

2 tbsp Liquid Aminos or tamari

2 cloves garlic, minced

1 tsp dried oregano

½ tsp smoked paprika

Salt and pepper, to taste

Avocado Spray

Fresh parsley or basil, chopped

DIRECTIONS

1. Preheat grill to medium-high heat.
2. In small bowl, whisk together balsamic vinegar, Liquid Aminos or tamari, garlic, oregano, smoked paprika, salt, and pepper.
3. Place eggplant in shallow dish or container, pour marinade over eggplant, and coat evenly. Let marinate, about 5-10 minutes, flipping once halfway through.
4. Lightly grease grill grates with avocado spray.
5. Grill, about 4-5 minutes per side, or until tender and grill marks appear, brushing with any remaining marinade as they cook.
6. Remove from grill, and transfer to serving platter. Garnish with fresh parsley or basil. Serve immediately.

HELPFUL TIPS

Grilling eggplant gives it a tender texture and adds a subtle smokiness, while the fresh parsley or basil garnish adds a burst of freshness. This dish is quick to prepare, making it perfect for summer barbecues or family get-togethers.

It doesn't have to be Tuesday to be Taco Night. This taco bar is perfect for family gatherings, offering a variety of plant-based options that are delicious and satisfying.

TACO BAR

PREP TIME: 30 MINUTES   **COOK TIME: 30 MINUTES**   **SERVINGS: 4**

INGREDIENTS

2 cups lentils, cooked

1 can (15 oz) black beans, drained and rinsed

1 cup corn

1 package taco seasoning mix

¾ cup water

Taco shells, corn or whole wheat

Optional Toppings:

1 bottle taco sauce

1 cup cherry tomatoes, halved

1 avocado, sliced

2 limes, cut into wedges

1 cup salsa

1 cup lettuce, shredded

1 cup red cabbage, shredded

½ cup black olives, sliced

½ cup red or yellow onion, chopped

Non-dairy shredded cheddar cheese

Non-dairy sour cream

¼ cup Jalapeños

DIRECTIONS

1. In a large fry pan, add lentils, beans, corn, taco seasoning, and water, and bring to boil.
2. Reduce heat and simmer, about 5 minutes.
3. Spoon taco mixture into taco shells.
4. Add favorite toppings from list. Serve immediately.

HELPFUL TIPS

Allow guests to assemble their own tacos using the prepared ingredients. Start with a taco shell and add desired fillings and toppings. Substitute taco shell with a bed of chopped lettuce.

Recipe contains nut by-products.*

Didn't use up all of your veggies this week? This mixture is the perfect solution for utilizing Mother Nature's Rainbow to help clean out the fridge.

VEGGIE GOULASH

PREP: 10 MIN   **COOK: 15 MIN**   **SERVES: 4**

INGREDIENTS

1 onion, diced

2 cloves garlic, minced

1 bell pepper, any color, diced

2 cups assorted vegetables, such as zucchini, carrots, mushrooms, chopped

1 can (15 oz) diced tomatoes

1 can (15 oz) kidney beans

1 tbsp tomato paste

2 cups vegetable broth + 1 tbsp

1 tsp dried oregano

1 tsp paprika

Salt and pepper, to taste

1 cup whole grain pasta, cooked

DIRECTIONS

1. In large pot, heat 1 tbsp broth over medium heat, add onion, and sauté, until translucent, about 3-4 minutes.
2. Stir in garlic and cook, about 2 minutes.
3. Add vegetables, and cook for 5-7 minutes, until softened.
4. Pour in diced tomatoes, beans, tomato paste, broth, dried oregano, paprika, salt, and pepper. Stir to combine.
5. Bring to boil, reduce heat to low, and simmer, about 15-20 minutes, stirring occasionally.
6. Serve immediately over pasta.

HELPFUL TIPS

Goulash *Definition: noun (gou·lash) A stew made with meat (not this time), assorted vegetables, and paprika. Perfect dish to freeze for a last minute meal.*

Slow Cooked Veggie Chili is my day off from cooking. A variety of beans and veggies, seasoned with rich spices, are cooked slowly to meld all the flavors together while I'm working. All I can say is yum!

SLOW COOKED VEGGIE CHILI

PREP: 15 MIN   COOK: 4-6 HOURS   SERVES: 8

INGREDIENTS

1 can (29 oz) tomato sauce

1 jar (16 oz) salsa

1 tbsp chili powder

1 package chili seasoning mix
(gluten-free option available)

1 can (15 oz) dark red kidney
beans, rinsed

1 can (15 oz) light red kidney
beans, rinsed

1 can (15 oz) black beans, rinsed

1 can (14.5 oz) diced tomatoes

1 bag (12 oz) frozen broccoli cuts

1 bag (12 oz) frozen carrots

1 bag (12 oz) frozen corn

1 cup mushrooms, chopped

¾ cup bell pepper, chopped

Non-dairy sour cream

Non-dairy cheddar cheese shreds

DIRECTIONS

1. In a slow cooker, pour in tomato sauce, salsa, chili powder, and chili seasoning mix, beans, tomatoes, broccoli, carrots, corn, mushrooms, and peppers. Stir to combine.
2. Cover, and set on low for 6 hours, or, if in a hurry, 4 hours on high.
3. Serve hot, and top with non-dairy sour cream and non-dairy cheddar cheese shreds.

HELPFUL TIPS

For an enhanced flavor, roast the mushrooms, peppers, and any other roasting-friendly vegetables in the oven before adding them to the chili. This step adds a delightful depth and complexity to the dish.

Be brave and experiment with different combinations. Change up your vegetables according to the season. All vegetables can work well together. Have fun.

ASIAN CAULIFLOWER RICE

PREP: 10 MIN   COOK: 10 MIN   SERVES: 4

INGREDIENTS

4 cups cauliflower rice

1½ cups vegetable broth

2 cups raw vegetables, chopped, such as mushrooms, onions, zucchini, carrots, broccoli, bok choy, sugar snap peas, water chestnuts, celery, and bell peppers

2 cups organic baby spinach

¼ cup Liquid Aminos or tamari

DIRECTIONS

1. In large fry pan, pour in ½ cup broth, and bring to boil. Add cauliflower rice and vegetables, cooking on high heat, about 2 minutes.
2. Add remaining broth, reduce to simmer, and cook until vegetables are 'al dente'.
3. Add organic baby spinach and Liquid Aminos or tamari, to taste. Serve immediately.

HELPFUL TIPS

Using frozen cauliflower rice saves time, and assures the vegetables do not become soggy. There should still be some vegetable broth left in the pan. If the veggies have soaked up all the broth, add a bit more to the pan and warm through.

A St Patrick's Day favorite, this old world recipe speaks for itself. I love how the lentils provide an excellent source of protein.

SHEPHERD'S PIE WITH LENTILS

PREP: 25 MIN   COOK: 1 HOUR 25 MIN   REST TIME: 10 MIN   SERVES: 6

INGREDIENTS

5 lbs red potatoes, peeled, diced, and cooked

½ cup non-dairy milk

3 tbsp non-diary butter

Salt and pepper, to taste

For Filling

1 medium yellow onion, diced

1½ tsp garlic, minced

1½ cups lentils, dried, rinsed and uncooked

4 cups vegetable broth +2 tbsp

1½ tsp dried thyme

1 cup frozen peas

10 oz bag frozen mixed vegetables

Avocado oil

DIRECTIONS

1. Preheat oven to 425°F.
2. In large bowl, mash potatoes with milk and butter. Salt and pepper.
3. In large saucepan, heat 2 tbsp broth over medium heat, and add onion and garlic. Sauté, about 5 minutes, until onion is translucent.
4. Stir in broth, lentils, and thyme. Add salt and pepper.
5. Bring mixture to boil, reduce heat, and simmer, about 30 minutes, until tender.
6. Add vegetables, and cook, about 10 minutes.
7. Grease 9x13 inch baking dish with avocado oil spray. Transfer mixture to baking dish.
8. Top with mashed potatoes, and spread evenly.
9. Bake for 15-20 minutes, until potatoes are lightly browned.
10. Allow to cool, about 5-10 minutes, and serve immediately.

HELPFUL TIPS

For more variety, try substituting potatoes with mashed cauliflower or sweet potatoes. Your family will love a thick layer of mashed potato.
***Recipe contains nut by-products.* ***

This plant-based gem has my husband eating his favorite meal again. Finding the non-dairy Ricotta Cheese combination is key to the taste of this dish. Mangia!

LASAGNA

PREP: 30 MIN   COOK: 1 HOUR   SERVES: 8

INGREDIENTS

1 can (15 oz) green lentils

2 jars (25 oz each) marinara sauce

1 tsp dried parsley

1 tsp dried rosemary

3 cups organic baby spinach

1 box whole grain or gluten-free lasagna noodles, uncooked

3 cups non-dairy mozzarella cheese, shredded

For Ricotta:

1 cup raw cashews

1 block (14½ oz) firm tofu, pressed

½ cup nutritional yeast

3 tbsp fresh lemon juice

1 tsp salt

¼ tsp dried basil

¼ tsp dried parsley

¼ tsp rosemary

1 tsp dried oregano

3 cloves garlic, minced

DIRECTIONS

1. Preheat oven to 350°F.
2. For Sauce, combine lentils, marinara sauce, parsley, and rosemary in a bowl.
3. For Ricotta, add cashews to food processor and process until fine. Add remaining ricotta ingredients, and pulse until smooth.
4. Evenly spread 1 cup sauce on bottom of casserole dish, and place 4-5 noodles on top.
5. Add half of the ricotta, and spread. Top with half of the spinach.
6. Evenly spread 1 cup of sauce over spinach, and place 4-5 noodles on top.
7. Add remaining ricotta, and spread. Top with remaining spinach.
8. Place 4-5 noodles on top of spinach, and evenly spread with remaining sauce.
9. Cover with foil, and bake for 40 minutes.
10. Remove foil, and top with cheese.
11. Bake uncovered for 20 minutes.
12. Allow to cool for 15 minutes before serving.

HELPFUL TIPS

To prepare BOLOGNESE style, add 1 cup plant-based ground beef to the sauce when cooking. Great meal to share with friends and family.

Recipe contains nuts and nut by-products.*

It's always fun to experiment with recipes customized to your taste. You can never get bored with so many different tasty possibilities. The most important thing to remember is to keep the ingredients whole and unprocessed.

MEDITERRANEAN QUINOA BOWL

PREP: 10 MIN   COOK: 20 MIN   SERVES: 4

INGREDIENTS

1 cup quinoa, cooked

1 can (15 oz) chickpeas, drained and rinsed

1 cup cherry tomatoes, halved

1 cucumber, diced

½ red onion, finely chopped

½ cup Kalamata olives, pitted and sliced

¼ cup fresh parsley, chopped

¼ cup fresh mint, chopped

½ cup non-dairy feta or parmesan cheese

For Dressing:

¼ cup avocado oil

2 tbsp lemon juice

1 tbsp red wine vinegar

1 tsp dried oregano

1 clove garlic

Salt and pepper, to taste

DIRECTIONS

1. In small bowl, whisk together all dressing ingredients.
2. Divide quinoa evenly among four bowls.
3. Top with chickpeas, cherry tomatoes, cucumber, red onion, Kalamata olives, parsley, mint, and cheese.
4. Pour on dressing and serve immediately, or refrigerate for up to 2 days.

HELPFUL TIPS

Customize with your favorite Mediterranean ingredients, such as Avocado slices, hummus, roasted red peppers, or artichoke hearts.

Recipe contains nut by-products.*

Use this low calorie, nutrient-dense vessel to carry a warm, flavorful manifest of veggie cargo. Bon Voyage!

ZUCCHINI BOATS

PREP: 15 MIN   COOK: 20-25 MIN   SERVES: 4

INGREDIENTS

4 medium zucchinis, halved lengthwise

1 cup quinoa or brown rice, cooked

1 can (15 oz) black beans

1 cup corn

1 cup tomato, diced

½ cup bell pepper, diced

¼ cup red onion, diced

2 cloves garlic, minced

1 tsp cumin

1 tsp chili powder

Salt and pepper, to taste

½ cup shredded non-dairy cheese

Fresh cilantro or parsley

Lime wedges

DIRECTIONS

1. Preheat oven to 375°F.
2. Remove center of zucchinis, creating boats. Finely chop centers, and set aside.
3. In large bowl, combine quinoa or brown rice, black beans, corn, tomato, bell pepper, red onion, garlic, and zucchini centers.
4. Add cumin, chili powder, salt, and pepper, and mix well.
5. Place boats in baking dish, spoon in mixture, and top with cheese.
6. Cover baking dish with foil, and bake for 20-25 minutes, until zucchinis are tender and filling is heated through.
7. Remove from oven, and let cool slightly.
8. Top with cilantro or parsley, and serve with lime wedges.

HELPFUL TIPS

Double the filling mixture and save to fill an acorn squash later in the week.
Recipe contains nut by-products.*

This member of the winter squash family whisks me off to memories of a fireside view and a snowy evening. Not only full of vitamins, it's packed with magnesium and calcium that help maintain strong bones.

STUFFED ACORN SQUASH

PREP: 15 MIN　　　*COOK: 45 MIN*　　　*SERVES: 4*

INGREDIENTS

2 acorn squash, halved and seeded

1 cup brown rice, cooked

½ cup walnuts, chopped

¼ cup raisins

1 tsp dried thyme (or 1 tbsp fresh)

2 tbsp balsamic vinegar

1 tbsp Liquid Aminos or tamari

Salt and pepper, to taste

DIRECTIONS

1. Preheat oven to 400°F.
2. Place squash cut-side down on baking sheet lined with parchment paper. Bake for 30-35 minutes, or until tender.
3. In medium bowl, combine brown rice, walnuts, raisins, and thyme.
4. In small bowl, whisk together balsamic vinegar and Liquid Aminos or tamari.
5. Carefully flip squash, and divide rice mixture evenly in each half. Drizzle with dressing, and salt and pepper.
6. Return squash to oven, and bake for 10-15 minutes.
7. Allow to cool slightly before serving.

HELPFUL TIPS

The sweetness of acorn squash stuffed with this savory mixture makes a wonderful, warm, comforting meal.
Recipe contains nuts.*

I remind my clients to eat as much leafy greens as they can daily and to make spinach a mindful habit in everyday dishes. Spinach with Great Northern beans is a great way to help accomplish this.

GREENS & BEANS

PREP: 10 MIN   **COOK: 15 MIN**   **SERVES: 4**

INGREDIENTS

1 small onion, chopped

2 garlic cloves, minced

1 can (15 oz) Great Northern beans, drained and rinsed

1 lb organic baby spinach, chopped

½ cup vegetable broth + 2 tbsp

¼ cup almonds, slivered

Salt and pepper, to taste

DIRECTIONS

1. In large skillet, add 2 tbsp broth over medium heat, add onion, and sauté for 3-4 minutes, until translucent. Add garlic, and sauté for another 1-2 minutes, until fragrant.
2. Add beans, and stir well.
3. Add spinach, a handful at a time, stirring until wilted.
4. Pour in broth, stir, cover, and simmer, about 5-7 minutes.
5. Remove from heat, and season with salt and pepper. Serve topped with slivered almonds.

HELPFUL TIPS

This is a great meal, so don't be hesitant to double it up for leftovers. Try squeezing fresh lemon juice over the dish before serving for added brightness.
Recipe contains nuts.*

Try it without the non-dairy cheese for a different flavor experience. It's always fun to experiment with recipes by customizing them to your taste. Make your own pizza, and keep the ingredients as whole and unprocessed as possible.

PIZZA CREATIONS

PREP: 15 MIN   *COOK: 15 -20 MIN*   *SERVES: 4*

INGREDIENTS

1 whole grain or gluten-free pizza crust

1 can (8 oz) tomato sauce, or jar pizza sauce

1 tbsp oregano

1 tbsp garlic powder

1 tbsp onion powder

1 tbsp dried parsley

2 large handfuls organic baby spinach, chopped

Non-dairy shredded mozzarella cheese

1 tbsp Italian seasoning

Suggested Toppings:

Peppers

Onions

Green and black olives

Broccoli

Mushrooms

Tomatoes, sliced

Cauliflower

Artichokes

Capers

Asparagus

DIRECTIONS

1. Preheat oven according to pizza crust instructions.
2. Spread sauce on crust, and season with oregano, garlic powder, onion powder, and parsley. Top with spinach.
3. Add any combination of suggested toppings.
4. Sprinkle with cheese.
5. Top with additional oregano, parsley, and Italian seasoning.
6. Bake for 10-15 minutes, until crust is crunchy and cheese is melted.
7. Slice, serve, and enjoy.

HELPFUL TIPS

Look for no salt added, and low sugar pizza sauce when shopping.

Recipe contains nut by-products.*

Whole grains make this dish a more comforting and satiating choice. These simple, easy-to-make Stuffed Bell Peppers have almost limitless stuffing combinations.

STUFFED BELL PEPPERS

PREP: 10 MIN   COOK: 15 MIN   SERVES: 4

INGREDIENTS

4 large bell peppers, any color

¼ cup vegetable broth + 1 tbsp

1 tbsp garlic, minced

1 cup mushrooms, chopped

½ cup onion, chopped

2 cups brown rice or quinoa, cooked

1 can (29 oz) tomato sauce

1 can (14.5 oz) diced tomatoes

2 cups organic baby spinach, chopped

Italian seasoning, to taste

Non-dairy shredded cheddar cheese

DIRECTIONS

1. In large pot, fill peppers with water to prevent them from floating, and continue adding water until fully covered. Cover pot, and bring to boil. Lower heat and simmer, about 3 minutes, or until tender. Place in baking dish.
2. In medium skillet, heat 1 tbsp broth, sauté garlic, mushrooms, and onion, about 5 minutes, or until browned.
3. In large bowl, combine broth, rice, tomato sauce, diced tomatoes, spinach, and Italian seasoning.
4. Add skillet mixture to large bowl, and combine. Stuff peppers, and top with cheese.
5. Bake uncovered for 25-35 minutes, until heated through, and serve immediately.

HELPFUL TIPS

As always, feel free to add or take away additional veggies to rice mixture. It's always fun to experiment with recipes customizing to your favorite taste. Remember, your goal is to keep the ingredients as whole and unprocessed as possible.

Recipe contains nut by-products.*

Healthy Living Is A Journey, Not A Destination.

CHAPTER 5 SIDE DISHES

The delicious and satisfying Cauliflower Steak is one of my new favorites. The heart of the stalk becomes surprisingly tender and flavorful when baked or grilled. My hubby actually uses steak sauce on these beauties.

CAULIFLOWER STEAK

PREP: 10 MIN   COOK: 15 MIN   SERVES: 4

INGREDIENTS

1 large head cauliflower, trim stem, and cut into 1 inch slices

¼ cup vegetable broth

2 tbsp balsamic vinegar

2 tbsp Liquid Aminos or tamari

1 tbsp maple syrup

1 tsp Dijon mustard

1 tsp smoked paprika

½ tsp garlic powder

Salt and pepper, to taste

¼ cup capers

Fresh parsley, chopped

DIRECTIONS

1. Preheat oven to 425°F.
2. In small bowl, whisk together broth, balsamic vinegar, Liquid Aminos or tamari, maple syrup, mustard, smoked paprika, garlic powder, salt, and pepper.
3. Brush both sides of cauliflower with marinade, and place on baking sheet lined with parchment paper. Stuff capers into cauliflower crevices.
4. Bake for 10 minutes on each side. Broil for 1 minute to crisp.
5. Remove from oven, sprinkle with parsley, and serve warm as a main dish or as a hearty side dish.

HELPFUL TIPS

Try these cauliflower steaks wrapped in foil on the grill.

Give thanks all year round. This side dish can be enjoyed whenever the urge hits you. No need to wait for the holidays. Get your fiber and vitamins with this non-dairy Green Bean Casserole.

GREEN BEAN CASSEROLE

PREP: 15 MIN   COOK: 30 MIN   SERVES: 6

INGREDIENTS

1 lb fresh green beans, trimmed and cut

1 onion, sliced

2 cloves garlic, minced

8 oz mushrooms, fresh, sliced

1 cup vegetable broth + 1 tbsp

1 cup non-dairy milk

3 tbsp nutritional yeast

2 tbsp arrowroot

1 tsp Liquid Aminos or tamari

½ tsp dried thyme

½ tsp onion powder

Salt and pepper, to taste

1½ cups crispy fried onions

DIRECTIONS

1. Preheat oven to 375°F.
2. Bring large pot of water to boil. Add green beans, and blanch, about 3-4 minutes, until tender. Drain, rinse with cold water, and set aside.
3. In large skillet, add 1 tbsp broth, sauté onion until translucent, about 5 minutes. Add garlic and mushrooms, and cook for 5 minutes.
4. In small bowl, whisk together broth, milk, nutritional yeast, arrowroot, Liquid Aminos or tamari, dried thyme, onion powder, salt, and pepper, until smooth.
5. Add green beans and sauce to skillet, and stir to combine. Transfer to lightly greased baking dish. Cover with foil, and bake for 20 minutes.
6. Remove foil, and sprinkle with onions. Return to oven and bake, uncovered, for 10 minutes.

HELPFUL TIPS

Nutritional yeast adds a cheesy flavor without any dairy. Crispy fried onions on top provide a satisfying crunch.
Recipe contains nut by-products. *

This non-dairy Cheezy Broccoli Rice combines fiber-loaded brown rice with tender steamed broccoli, providing an antioxidant side dish the family will love. I've been known to double the portion and make it my meal.

CHEEZY BROCCOLI RICE

PREP: 10 MIN   COOK: 25 MIN   SERVES: 4

INGREDIENTS

1½ cups brown rice, uncooked

1 cup water

3 cups broccoli florets, chopped

1 cup non-dairy milk

½ cup nutritional yeast

1 tsp garlic powder

1 can (14 oz) coconut milk

Salt and pepper, to taste

DIRECTIONS

1. Combine all ingredients in rice cooker or Insta-Pot.
2. Cook using the standard "Rice" function.

HELPFUL TIPS

Serve this Cheezy Broccoli Rice warm as a delicious and nutritious side dish or a light main course.

Recipe contains nut by-products.*

No added sugars in this recipe. Enjoy the natural sweetness these potatoes provide. Such a delightful blend of sweet and savory flavors.

SWEET POTATO BAKE

PREP: 10 MIN   *COOK: 20 - 25 MIN*   *SERVES: 4*

INGREDIENTS

2 medium sweet potatoes,
peeled and cubed

1 tbsp maple syrup

1 tsp ground cinnamon

Pinch of salt

Avocado oil spray

DIRECTIONS

1. Preheat oven to 400°F.
2. Place potatoes on baking sheet lined with parchment paper, and lightly spray with avocado spray.
3. Bake for 20-25 minutes, or until tender and slightly caramelized, tossing halfway through. Remove from oven, and transfer to bowl.
4. Drizzle with maple syrup, sprinkle with cinnamon, and add a pinch of salt. Toss gently to coat, and serve warm.

HELPFUL TIPS

This is a perfect dish to freeze for leftovers. Reheats nicely in the microwave oven.

Fresh ingredients are key to creating this low fat, fiber-full guacamole recipe. Get creative and slice carrots, cucumbers, celery, peppers, and zucchini to use as your dipping tools. These veggies provide more nutrients and less calories than chips.

FRESH GUACAMOLE

PREP: 15 MIN   *COOK: NONE*   *SERVES: 8*

INGREDIENTS

6 avocados, cut in half and pit removed

1 lime, fresh

½ tsp garlic powder

¼ cup fresh cilantro, chopped

½ tsp sea salt

½ cup yellow onion, finely chopped

2 large tomatoes, chopped

DIRECTIONS

1. In medium bowl, mash avocados to desired consistency, and squeeze in lime juice. Add garlic powder, cilantro, and salt, and gently stir to combine.
2. Fold in onion and tomato, and transfer to a serving dish.
3. Serve with tortilla chips, on tacos, or as a topping for salads.

HELPFUL TIPS

Place the seeds of the avocado in the guacamole to help maintain the green color.

When you need that extra side dish, this Spanish Rice cooks up quickly and easily, providing you with that other option. Fill up with fiber.

SPANISH RICE

PREP: 10 MIN   **COOK: 20 MIN**   **SERVES: 6**

INGREDIENTS

1 small onion, finely chopped

2 cloves garlic, minced

1 red bell pepper, diced

4 cups brown rice, cooked

1 can (15 oz) diced tomatoes, drained

1 can (8 oz) tomato sauce

2 tbsp Mexican spice blend (see page 191)

2 tbsp water

Salt and pepper, to taste

Fresh cilantro, chopped

DIRECTIONS

1. In large skillet, heat water over medium heat, add onion, and cook until translucent, about 5 minutes.
2. Add garlic and bell pepper, and cook until softened.
3. Stir in rice, tomatoes, tomato sauce, and Mexican spice blend, and heat, about 5-10 minutes, stirring occasionally.
4. Season with salt and pepper. Garnish with cilantro, and serve.

HELPFUL TIPS

You can add cooked beans, corn, or peas for additional flavor and nutrition. Store any leftovers in an airtight container in the refrigerator for up to 3 days.

For the love of potatoes. These seasoned wedges make a scrumptious addition to any meal. Say goodbye to fried potatoes, and hello to the healing benefits of a natural potato. A great choice as a favorite complex carbohydrate.

AUNT KK FRIES

PREP: 15 MIN   COOK: 45 MIN   SERVES: 4

INGREDIENTS

4 large Russet potatoes, cut
lengthwise into ½ inch wedges

Avocado oil spray

Sea salt

Garlic power

Italian seasoning

DIRECTIONS

1. Preheat oven to 400°F.
2. On a baking sheet lined with parchment paper, arrange potatoes in a single layer, and spray with avocado oil.
3. Season with salt, garlic powder, and Italian seasoning.
4. Bake for 30 minutes, flip, and cook an additional 15 minutes, or until golden brown.
5. Broil until crispy, checking often to prevent burning.
6. Serve immediately with your favorite dipping sauce.

HELPFUL TIPS

Combine two side dishes, like Cauliflower Steak and Aunt KK fries, for a terrific meal. Perfect for a quick snack or a hearty side dish.

A fabulous protein and hydration boost for your meal. Delight in the rich flavors of Sautéed Mushrooms with garlic and onions. It pairs perfectly as a side or topping for baked potato, pasta, or sandwich.

SAUTÉED MUSHROOMS

PREP: 10 MIN   COOK: 15 MIN   SERVES: 4

INGREDIENTS

2 tbsp vegetable broth

½ lb Baby Portobello mushrooms, sliced

½ lb Cremini mushrooms, sliced

1 large onion, thinly sliced

4 cloves garlic, minced

Salt and pepper, to taste

1 tbsp fresh thyme

DIRECTIONS

1. In large skillet, heat broth over medium-high heat, add mushrooms, and cook, stirring occasionally, until tender.
2. Add onions, stirring occasionally, until caramelized, about 5-7 minutes.
3. Stir in garlic, and cook, about 1-2 minutes, until fragrant.
4. Season with salt and pepper.
5. Remove from heat, garnish with thyme, and serve.

HELPFUL TIPS

Enjoy these mushrooms, with their natural juices, over baked potatoes. Be sure to make more to have on hand for other meals.

No more boiled Brussels sprouts. Indulge in the delightful flavors as a savory side dish that marries the earthy essence of Brussels sprouts with the aromatic blend of garlic, Italian seasoning, and oregano.

ROASTED BRUSSELS SPROUTS

PREP: 10 MIN   *COOK: 15 MIN*   *SERVES: 4*

INGREDIENTS

1 lb Brussels sprouts, halved

Avocado oil spray

2 tbsp garlic powder

2 tbsp Italian seasoning

1 tbsp dried oregano

Salt and pepper, to taste

DIRECTIONS

1. Preheat oven to 400°F.
2. Line baking sheet with parchment paper, spread Brussels sprouts in single layer, and lightly spray with avocado oil spray.
3. Season with garlic powder, Italian seasoning, oregano, salt, and pepper.
4. Roast for 20-25 minutes, or until tender, stirring halfway through.
5. Broil until crispy, checking often to prevent burning.
6. Serve immediately.

HELPFUL TIPS

Adjust seasoning to your taste preference. You can add more garlic powder, Italian seasoning, or additional herbs for extra flavor. Avocado spray helps in achieving a crispy texture while keeping the recipe low oil.

Plant-Based

It's

A Green Thing

CHAPTER 6 SOUPS & BROTH

This is easier than you think. Create this nutritious Fresh Veggie Broth using your vegetable scraps. Save yourself tons of calories, and replace the majority of oils normally used in recipes. You can enhance the nutrients in cooking by replacing water with broth.

FRESH VEGGIE BROTH

PREP: 20 MIN   ***COOK: 2 HOURS***   ***COOLING TIME: 4 HOURS***

INGREDIENTS

Vegetable scraps - ends, clippings, stems, peelings - from celery, bell peppers, carrots, onions, spinach, broccoli, cauliflower

DIRECTIONS

1. Add scraps to medium-sized brown bag, and line bottom with paper towel. Continue to add scraps when preparing vegetables. Can be stored in refrigerator for up to one week.
2. When ready to cook, transfer scraps into large stock pot, and fill with water, leaving about two inches from top.
3. Cover, and bring to boil. Reduce heat, and simmer for 4 hours, stirring occasionally, until vegetables are soft. Turn off heat, and cool completely.
4. Place colander over large bowl in sink, use ladle to scoop vegetables into colander, and press with potato masher. Repeat until all broth is extracted.
5. Put into jar or container, and store in refrigerator for up to one week, or in freezer for up to three months.

HELPFUL TIPS

Avoid strong-flavored or spicy vegetables like jalapeños, onion or radish leaves. Use this fresh veggie broth for soups, sauteing, or to add additional flavor to a recipe that calls for water.

This Creamy Bean Soup features some whole food all-stars. Protein, fiber, non-dairy, and low fat team up to make a flavorful soup that's both wholesome and creamy.

CREAMY BEAN SOUP

PREP: 20 MIN   *COOK: 30 MIN*   *SERVES: 8*

INGREDIENTS

8 cups vegetable broth

1 cup carrots, diced

1 cup celery, diced

1 cup peas, frozen

1 medium red onion, chopped

2 cups organic baby spinach, chopped

2 cups mushrooms, chopped

1 cup broccoli, chopped

2 cans (15 oz each) white beans, drained and rinsed

¼ cup raw cashews

½ cup nutritional yeast

Salt and pepper, to taste

DIRECTIONS

1. In large stock pot, heat broth over medium-high heat, until boiling.
2. Add carrots, celery, peas, onion, spinach, mushrooms, broccoli, and white beans to pot. Reduce heat, and simmer, about 20-25 minutes.
3. Combine cashews and nutritional yeast in a high-powered blender, and blend on high, until a fine powder.
4. Add 2 cups soup to blender, and blend on high, until creamy and smooth. Add mixture to stock pot, stirring well to incorporate. Simmer for an additional 5 minutes, and season with salt and pepper.
5. Serve hot.

HELPFUL TIPS

A squeeze of fresh lemon or lime juice can enhance the flavors and add a touch of brightness.

Recipe contains nuts and nut by-products.*

This comforting Vegetable Soup offers a bounty of antioxidant goodness, from Mother Nature's rainbow of veggies, including mushrooms, tender carrots, broccoli, crunchy celery, sweet bell peppers, and many others.

VEGETABLE SOUP

PREP: 20 MIN   COOK: 30 MIN   SERVES: 6

INGREDIENTS

6 cups vegetable broth

2 cups each - carrots, broccoli, celery, bell peppers, chopped

1 cup yellow zucchini, chopped

½ cup onion, chopped

1 cup frozen peas

1 can (15 oz) beans of choice, drained and rinsed

4 cloves garlic

4 bay leaves

1 tbsp dried parsley

1 tbsp smoked paprika

1 can (12 oz) diced tomatoes

DIRECTIONS

1. Pour broth into stock pot, and add remaining ingredients.
2. Bring to boil.
3. Cover, and simmer for 30 minutes.
4. Serve hot.

HELPFUL TIPS

Use frozen or fresh vegetables. Eat soup as is or add pasta, but keep the pasta separate from soup until ready to serve to avoid the pasta soaking up the broth. Always cook gluten-free or whole wheat pastas separately.

This low calorie soup is rich in selenium and B vitamins. The combination of Oyster, Bella, and Cremini mushrooms provides a rich, earthy flavor while contributing to the nutritional value of the soup. This recipe turned me into a true fan.

MUSHROOM SOUP

PREP: 15 MIN   COOK: 15 MIN   SERVES: 4

INGREDIENTS

1 cup each - Oyster, Bella, and
Cremini mushrooms, chopped
1 medium onion, chopped
3 cloves garlic, chopped
1 medium carrot, chopped
2 celery stalks, chopped
1 tsp dried rosemary
1 tsp dried thyme
Salt and pepper, to taste
4 cups vegetable broth + ¼ cup
1 cup coconut milk
1 tsp fresh parsley

DIRECTIONS

1. In large stock pot, heat ¼ cup broth over medium heat, and add onion, garlic, carrot, and celery. Sauté, about 5 minutes.
2. Add mushrooms, and cook, about 5-7 minutes.
3. Add rosemary and thyme. Season with salt and pepper.
4. Pour in remaining broth, and bring to boil. Reduce heat, and let simmer, about 15 minutes.
5. Stir in coconut milk, and let simmer, about 5 minutes.
6. For creamier texture, use an immersion blender, and blend until smooth.
7. Garnish with fresh parsley, and serve.

HELPFUL TIPS

For a little variety, add two cups of chopped Russet potatoes to make it even more nutritious and satisfying.
Recipe contains nut by-products.*

Next to my Plant-Based Lasagna, this creamy, comforting, and delicious Boston Clam Chowder is my hubby's new favorite soup...and most importantly, it's dairy-free.

BOSTON CLAM CHOWDER

PREP: 15 MIN   COOK: 50 MIN   SERVES: 4

INGREDIENTS

1 cup non-dairy milk

½ cup raw cashews

1 large yellow onion, diced

3 cloves garlic, minced

2 medium carrots, chopped

3 celery stalks, diced

4 medium potatoes, peeled and diced

2 bay leaves

1 tsp dried thyme

1 tsp dried dill

1 tsp smoked paprika

2 tsp Dulse flakes

½ tbsp lemon, juiced

Salt and pepper, to taste

4 cups vegetable broth + 2 tbsp

1 cup Oyster mushrooms

3 tbsp almond flour mixed with 2 tbsp water

2 tbsp fresh parsley, chopped

DIRECTIONS

1. In high-powered blender, mix milk and cashews, until smooth.
2. In large stock pot, heat 2 tbsp broth over medium heat, and add onion and garlic. Sauté, about 5 minutes.
3. Add carrots and celery, sauté, about 5 minutes, and stir in potatoes, bay leaves, thyme, dill, smoked paprika, Dulse flakes, lemon juice, salt, and pepper. Cook for 3 minutes.
4. Pour in broth, bring to boil, reduce heat, and simmer for 20 minutes.
5. Add mushrooms, and simmer for 5 minutes.
6. Stir flour mixture into soup to thicken, and cook for 5 minutes, stirring continuously.
7. Garnish with parsley, and serve.

HELPFUL TIPS

Try this soup in a whole grain bread bowl. The dulse flakes and oyster mushrooms give the chowder it's seafood flavor.
Recipe contains nuts and nut by-products.*

A lovely summer refresher for lunchtime or anytime, this soup will cool you off on a hot summer day, while leaving your taste buds dancing with flavor. Loaded with healthy fats to keep you satiated, while the cucumber provides much needed hydration.

AVO-CUCUMBER SOUP

PREP: 10 MIN   COOK: 15 MIN   SERVES: 4   REFRIGERATE: 2 HRS

INGREDIENTS

2 large avocados, pitted

1 cucumber, seeded and cut into chunks

½ cup fresh cilantro, packed

1 Jalapeno pepper, seeded

1 tsp of salt

2 tsp ground cumin

3 large garlic cloves

2½ tsp ground coriander

½ cup non-dairy coconut yogurt

1 lime, juiced

1¾ cups cold water

¾ cup peas, cooked

DIRECTIONS

1. In blender, combine all ingredients, except for ½ cup peas, and blend on high, until smooth. If soup is too thick, add more yogurt or cold water.
2. Stir in remaining peas.
3. Refrigerate for at least 2 hours.
4. Serve chilled.

HELPFUL TIPS

This soup can be left in the fridge for up to two days before serving. This simple, refreshing, light meal can be served with whole grain bread, crackers, or a fruit salad. Perfect meal on a hot summer day.

Recipe contains nut by-products*

Who said soup can only be eaten for lunch or dinner?
Start your morning meal with this yummy hot soup.
Garnish with toasted pumpkin seeds or fresh herbs,
and enjoy this creamy non-dairy soup.

CREAMY BROCCOLI SOUP

PREP: 10 MIN   COOK: 25 MIN   SERVES: 4

INGREDIENTS

1 onion, diced

3 cloves garlic, minced

4 cups broccoli, chopped

1 can (14 oz) coconut milk

2 cups vegetable broth + 1 tbsp

1 tsp ground turmeric

1 tsp ground cumin

Salt and pepper, to taste

1 lemon, juiced

DIRECTIONS

1. In large stock pot, heat 1 tbsp broth over medium heat, and add onion and garlic. Sauté, about 3-4 minutes.
2. Add broccoli, and cook, about 3-4 minutes, stirring occasionally.
3. Stir in coconut milk, broth, turmeric, cumin, and bring to boil.
4. Reduce heat, and simmer, about 15-20 minutes, or until broccoli is tender.
5. Using an immersion blender or blender, mix until smooth and creamy.
6. Season with salt and pepper.
7. Top with lemon juice, and serve immediately.

HELPFUL TIPS

Love to pour over a baked potato. For a richer texture, blend in a tbsp of nutritional yeast or a splash of non-dairy milk (like almond or oat milk) before serving.Optional toppings: toasted pumpkin seeds, chopped fresh herbs.
Recipe contains nut by-products.*

Invest In Your Health One Bite At A Time!

CHAPTER 7   SALADS

This non-dairy Caprese Salad is packed with many essential nutrients. Enjoy this plant-based rendition as a light and refreshing lunch or appetizer, perfect for summer gatherings or any time you crave a healthy, flavorful salad.

CAPRESE SALAD

PREP: 15 MIN   *SERVES: 4*

INGREDIENTS

1 block (14 oz) extra firm tofu, pressed, drained, and cubed

2 cups cherry tomatoes, sliced and seeded

Fresh basil leaves, torn

Balsamic glaze

Salt and pepper, to taste

Feta Chez Marinade:

3 tbsp lemon juice

½ lemon, thinly sliced

2 tbsp apple cider vinegar

¼ cup vegetable broth

1 tsp dried oregano

1 tsp dried rosemary

1 tsp garlic powder

1 tsp onion powder

1 tsp dried dill

1 tsp salt

DIRECTIONS

1. In small bowl, whisk together all marinade ingredients.
2. Place tofu in shallow dish or ball jar, and add marinade to ensure all pieces are coated.
3. Refrigerate covered for at least 1 hour to allow flavors to meld. Overnight is best.
4. On serving platter, alternate tomato, feta, and basil.
5. Season with salt and pepper.
6. Just before serving, drizzle with balsamic glaze.

HELPFUL TIPS

For a slightly different presentation, try serving on a skewer.

Do you crave crunch? Taste this refreshing salad bursting with antioxidants in colors from the veggie rainbow. You'll find a fiber powerhouse and a real crowd pleaser in the Raw and Radiant Salad.

RAW AND RADIANT SALAD

PREP: 20 MIN   *SERVES: 4*

INGREDIENTS

1 head red cabbage, sliced

1 large carrot, grated

1 red bell pepper, sliced

1 cucumber, sliced

1 cup snow peas, halved

½ cup edamame beans, shelled

¼ cup fresh cilantro leaves, torn

1 radish, sliced

¼ cup fresh mint leaves, torn

¼ cup roasted peanuts, chopped

2 tbsp sesame seeds

For Dressing:

3 tbsp Liquid Aminos or tamari

2 tbsp rice vinegar

1 tbsp sesame oil

1 tbsp maple syrup or honey

1 tsp fresh ginger, grated

1 clove garlic, minced

1 lime, juiced

DIRECTIONS

1. In large bowl, combine cabbage, carrot, pepper, cucumber, snow peas, edamame, cilantro, radish, and mint.
2. In small bowl, whisk together dressing ingredients.
3. Pour over vegetables, and toss well to coat.
4. Top with peanuts and sesame seeds.
5. Serve immediately.

HELPFUL TIPS

This Raw and Radiant Salad adds an Asian flair to the typical salad. If you're looking for a little more "heat" try adding Wasabi or red pepper flakes to the dressing.
Recipe contains nuts.*

Using the ingredients in this recipe can help lower inflammation. Cut your preparation time by using the base of a packaged coleslaw mix. It's a win-win. This recipe makes the perfect companion to many of the other recipes in my book.

COLESLAW

PREP: 10 MIN   COOK: 15 MIN   SERVES: 4

INGREDIENTS

1 bag (16 oz) packaged coleslaw

¼ cup red onion, thinly sliced

⅓ cup vegan mayonnaise

1 tbsp maple syrup

2 tbsp seasoned rice vinegar

2 tbsp fresh dill, chopped

Salt and pepper, to taste

DIRECTIONS

1. In large bowl, combine coleslaw and onion.
2. In jar, add mayonnaise, maple syrup, vinegar, dill, salt, and pepper, cover tightly, and shake until well blended.
3. Pour dressing over coleslaw and onion, and toss until thoroughly combined.
4. Serve immediately.

HELPFUL TIPS

Serve this coleslaw on top of my Bean Burger (see page 70) or Carrot Hot Dogs (see page 72) recipes. Perfect as a summer side dish. Buy the coleslaw packages without the prepackaged dressing.

Recipe contains nut by-products*

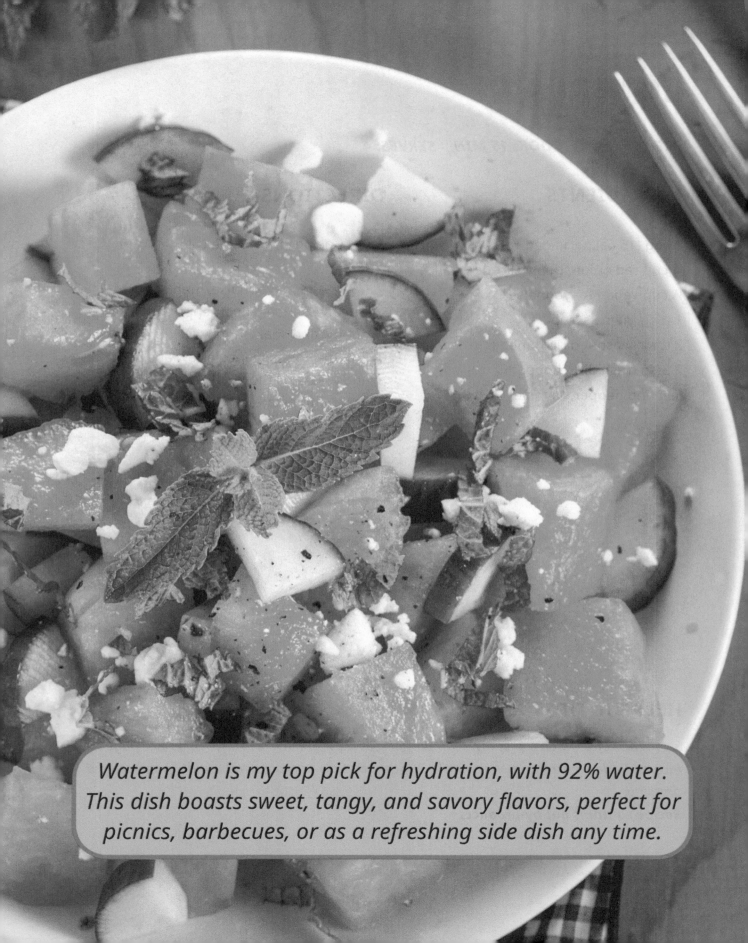

Watermelon is my top pick for hydration, with 92% water. This dish boasts sweet, tangy, and savory flavors, perfect for picnics, barbecues, or as a refreshing side dish any time.

WATERMELON SALAD

PREP: 15 MIN   CHILL: 30 MIN   SERVES: 6

INGREDIENTS

1 medium watermelon, chopped

2 cucumbers, chopped

1 large red onion, chopped

½ cup non-dairy feta cheese, crumbled (see page 145)

For Marinade:

½ cup maple syrup or honey

¼ cup balsamic vinegar

2 tsp garlic powder

1 lemon, juiced

1 lime, juiced

½ tsp fresh mint, chopped

½ tsp fresh basil, chopped

DIRECTIONS

1. In large bowl, whisk together marinade ingredients.
2. Add watermelon, and toss gently to coat. Refrigerate for 30 minutes to allow flavors to meld.
3. Add cucumber and red onion, and mix to combine.
4. Sprinkle with cheese, and serve immediately.

HELPFUL TIPS

For different flavor variations, experiment with different spices or herbs, such as chili powder or basil, to suit your taste. Enjoy this refreshing and flavorful Watermelon Salad as a delightful side dish or a light summer meal.

More of a meal than a side dish, this beauty combines bite-sized al dente pasta with a colorful assortment of fresh vegetables. No added sugars in this dish, my friends.

PASTA SALAD

PREP: 10 MIN   COOK: 10 MIN   SERVES: 6

INGREDIENTS

1 package (8 oz) pasta, whole grain or gluten-free, cooked

1 cup cherry tomatoes, halved

1 cup cucumber, chopped

1 cup non-dairy mozzarella cheese

½ cup red bell pepper, chopped

¼ cup red onion, chopped

¼ cup fresh parsley, chopped

¼ cup fresh basil, chopped

For Dressing:

1 ripe avocado

¼ cup lemon, juiced

2 tbsp water

1 tbsp Dijon mustard

1 clove garlic

Salt and pepper, to taste

DIRECTIONS

1. In large bowl, combine pasta, tomato, cucumber, ½ cup cheese, pepper, onion, parsley, and basil.
2. In blender or food processor, mix all dressing ingredients, until smooth and creamy.
3. Pour dressing over pasta and vegetables, toss until well coated, and top with ½ cup cheese.
4. Serve immediately.

HELPFUL TIPS

This can be made ahead of time, and can be stored in the refrigerator. Customize by adding other vegetables, such as olives, artichoke hearts, or roasted peppers. Garnish with additional fresh herbs or a sprinkle of nutritional yeast for extra flavor.

This recipe contains nut by-products

Boost your vitamin C to the next level with this Citrus Salad. Enhanced with a gently-simmered syrup of honey, lemon zest, and vanilla, this one's worth a try.

CITRUS SALAD

PREP: 15 MIN   COOK: 10 MIN   SERVES: 4

INGREDIENTS

1 large lemon, zest into long strips, and juiced

¼ cup honey or maple syrup

3 tbsp water

1 tsp vanilla extract or 1 vanilla bean

1 navel orange, peeled and sliced

1 blood orange, peeled and sliced

1 clementine, peeled and sliced

1 tangerine, peeled and sliced

2 kiwi, peeled and sliced

1 pink grapefruit, peeled and sliced

1 tbsp mint

¼ cup pomegranate seeds

¼ walnuts or pecans, chopped

DIRECTIONS

1. To make syrup, combine zest, honey, water, vanilla, and 1 tbsp lemon juice in a small saucepan over medium heat.
2. Simmer, about 5-8 minutes, until slightly thickened. Stir occasionally, and remove from heat. Strain to remove zest and vanilla bean, if used.
3. Place sliced fruit in large bowl, add syrup, and gently toss to coat.
4. Garnish with mint, pomegranate seeds, and walnuts or pecans.
5. Serve chilled or at room temperature.

HELPFUL TIPS

Enjoy the refreshing and vibrant flavors of this Citrus Salad. Feel free to adjust the ingredients to include more of your favorite ingredients.
Recipe contains nuts.*

Foods:
Whole
Fresh Clean

CHAPTER 8 DRESSINGS

No surprise that this dressing is loaded with vitamin C. For those who love sauces like I do, use this for drizzling over greens, as a marinade, or over whole grain pasta, just to name a few.

CITRUS SALAD DRESSING

PREP: 10 MIN   *SERVES: 4*

INGREDIENTS

1 cup fresh orange juice

4 tbsp fresh lemon juice

4 tbsp fresh lime juice

4 cloves garlic, minced

4 tbsp Dijon mustard

4 tbsp honey or maple syrup

½ cup water

½ tsp salt

½ tsp pepper

DIRECTIONS

1. In small bowl, combine all ingredients, and whisk together, until well blended and smooth.
2. Enjoy on your favorite salad.

HELPFUL TIPS

Use immediately to dress your favorite salad or store in a sealed container in the refrigerator for up to one week.

Never in my wildest dreams could I ever have imagined peanut butter as a salad dressing. Don't knock it until you try it. All I can say is, WOW!

PEANUT BUTTER DRESSING

PREP: 10 MIN   *SERVES: 4*

INGREDIENTS

¼ cup organic peanut butter

¼ cup coco or coconut aminos

2 tbsp apple cider vinegar

Pinch of sea salt and pepper

DIRECTIONS

1. Mix all ingredients, using fork or small whisk, until smooth and creamy.
2. Enjoy on salads or mixture of shredded cabbage.

HELPFUL TIPS

Experience the rich and nutty flavors to elevate your salad. If you can, use organic peanut butter. Try both smooth and crunchy for variety.

Recipe contains nuts and nut by-product.*

The healthy fats and antioxidants in avocado can help reduce inflammation. You will see a few avocados on my kitchen counter ready for use at all times.

AVOCADO DRESSING

PREP: 10 MIN　　　**SERVES: 4**

INGREDIENTS

1 avocado

Pinch of garlic powder

¼ cup lime juice

Pinch of salt

DIRECTIONS

1. In blender or food processor, combine all ingredients, and blend, until smooth and creamy.
2. Enjoy over chopped kale or spinach.

HELPFUL TIPS

Pour it over chopped kale and spinach, then massage it into the greens to coat them evenly. Enhance your sauce with your favorite raw veggies, mandarin orange slices, Craisins, and almonds for added fiber and a flavor burst. I like to triple this recipe to keep some on hand.

Almond butter is a plant-based source of protein, making this dressing a wonderful option after a workout. Pour over cut up raw veggies as a snack.

ALMOND BUTTER DRESSING

INGREDIENTS

¼ cup coco or coconut aminos

2 tbsp almond butter

2 tbsp lime, juiced

1 tsp ginger

1 tbsp pure maple syrup

DIRECTIONS

1. Mix all ingredients, using a fork or small whisk, until smooth and creamy.
2. Enjoy on salads or as a dip for fresh vegetables.

HELPFUL TIPS

Almond butter dressing can be customized with various seasonings and ingredients, allowing you to create a dressing that compliments a wide range of dishes and cuisines.
Recipe contains nut by-products.*

Made with wholesome ingredients, such as Dijon mustard, this dressing provides a balance of healthy fats and vitamins, making it a nutritious and versatile addition to your meals.

MUSTARD DRESSING

PREP: 10 MIN   **SERVES: 1**

INGREDIENTS

¼ cup Dijon mustard

1 tsp yellow mustard

1 tbsp white vinegar or apple
cider vinegar

1 tbsp lemon, juiced

½ avocado

¼ cup nutritional yeast

DIRECTIONS

1. Mix all ingredients, using a fork or small whisk, until smooth and creamy.
2. Enjoy on salads or mixture of shredded cabbage.

HELPFUL TIPS

This mixture can be used as a flavorful dressing, dip, or spread, providing a nutritious alternative to conventional condiments. Double the recipe and save some for another meal.

Anytime we can enjoy a creamy dressing that's non-dairy, it's a win-win for all. This is one of my family's favorite dressings. We use it as a dip as well.

RANCH DRESSING

PREP: 10 MIN   ***CHILL TIME: 3-4 HOURS***   ***SERVES: 6***

INGREDIENTS

1½ cups vegan mayonnaise

¼ cup non-dairy milk

1½ tsp apple cider vinegar

4 cloves garlic, minced

1 tbsp dried parsley

1 tsp dried dill

1 tsp onion powder

1 tsp sweet paprika

1 tsp fresh chives (or ½ tsp dried)

1 tbsp lemon, juiced

¼ tsp black pepper

Salt, to taste

DIRECTIONS

1. Mix all ingredients, using a fork or small whisk, until smooth and creamy.
2. Chill, about 3-4 hours, before using. This is essential for the flavors to meld together.
3. Serve on your favorite salad or as a dip for fresh vegetables.

HELPFUL TIPS

For a thicker dressing or dip, eliminate the plant-based milk and increase the vegan mayo to 2 cups.

Recipe contains nut by-products*

Believe In Yourself

CHAPTER 9 SAUCES & DIPS

This Bean Dip is a favorite "go-to" dip for me. It's quick to prepare and perfect for gatherings or snacking. Always a party when enjoying its vibrant flavors and wholesome ingredients.

BEAN DIP

PREP: 10 MIN   *SERVES: 4-6*

INGREDIENTS

½ cup onion, chopped

½ cup bell pepper, any color, chopped

1 tsp water

1 can (15 oz) black or pinto beans, drained and rinsed

1 cup salsa

½ cup organic corn (optional)

¼ cup shredded non-dairy taco cheese

DIRECTIONS

1. In blender or food processor, combine onion, pepper, and water.
2. Add beans and salsa. Pulse, until desired consistency is reached.
3. Place in small bowl, stir in corn, if using, and top with cheese.
4. Serve with whole grain tortilla chips or your favorite veggie dippers.

HELPFUL TIPS

I've made this with just beans and salsa in a pinch and used a potato masher. This dip goes great with celery, cucumber, zucchini slices, whole grain, or gluten-free crackers or chips.

Mushrooms contain roughly 92% water, creating hydration that helps maintain healthy skin. Savory and comforting, this sauce is perfect for those seeking a gluten-free, dairy-free, and oil-free alternative.

MUSHROOM GRAVY

PREP: 10 MIN   COOK: 20 MIN   MAKES: 2 CUPS

INGREDIENTS

2 cups mushrooms, Button or
Cremini, sliced

1 small onion, finely chopped

2 cloves garlic, minced

2 tbsp Liquid Aminos or tamari

2 cups vegetable broth

2 tbsp arrowroot

Salt and pepper, to taste

Fresh thyme or parsley

DIRECTIONS

1. In medium saucepan, dry-sauté mushrooms over medium heat, until moisture is released, about 3-5 minutes.
2. Add onion and garlic. Cook until onion is translucent, about 3-4 minutes.
3. Add Liquid Aminos or tamari, stir, and cook for 1 minute.
4. In small bowl, whisk together broth and arrowroot, until smooth. Pour into saucepan, stirring constantly.
5. Bring to simmer, about 5-7 minutes, stirring frequently, until thickened.
6. Season with salt and pepper.
7. Garnish with thyme or parsley, and serve.

HELPFUL TIPS

Serve over mashed potatoes, roasted vegetables, or any dish of your choice, for a satisfying and flavorful addition to your meal. Store any leftovers in an airtight container in the refrigerator for up to 3 days. Reheat gently on the stovetop or in the microwave before serving.

Chickpeas are a source of fiber, B vitamins and selenium. That's why these little gems are a staple in so many of my recipes. Being the sauce lover I am, I pour this over everything.

CHICKPEA SAUCE

PREP: 10 MIN   COOK: 15 MIN   SERVES: 4

INGREDIENTS

1 large shallot, chopped

1 jar (8½ oz) sun-dried tomatoes, drained and chopped

1½ tsp garlic, minced

2 cans (15 oz each) chickpeas, drained and rinsed

1 cup vegetable broth + ¼ cup

1 tsp paprika

1 tsp Italian seasoning

½ cup coconut milk

2 tbsp fresh basil, chopped

⅔ cup non-dairy Parmesan cheese (see page 179)

DIRECTIONS

1. In large skillet, sauté shallot in ¼ cup of broth over medium heat, until softened.
2. Add sun-dried tomatoes, garlic, chickpeas, remaining broth, paprika, and Italian seasoning. Bring to boil, reduce heat to medium-low, and simmer for 3 minutes, stirring occasionally.
3. Add to blender, and blend on high, until creamy and smooth. Add back to skillet.
4. Stir in coconut milk and basil. Simmer, until bubbling around edges.
5. Remove from heat, and stir in cheese.
6. Serve over whole grain or gluten-free bread, or baked sweet potato.

HELPFUL TIPS

Fresh basil adds a touch of brightness before finishing with a sprinkle of non-dairy Parmesan cheese. A comforting and delicious experience. Try it over your favorite pasta.

Let your creativity guide you. A non-dairy solution to the question: "What can I dip this in". Watch out nacho cheese world...there's a new player in town.

NACHO CHEEZ SAUCE

PREP: 10 MIN   ***MAKES 2 CUPS***

INGREDIENTS

1 cup raw cashews, soaked
overnight, drained, and rinsed

1 lemon, juiced

¾ cup nutritional yeast

⅓ cup water

1 tsp salt

1 tsp dried Jalapeno or Cayenne
pepper

1½ tsp garlic powder

½ tsp cumin

DIRECTIONS

1. In blender, combine cashews, lemon juice, nutritional yeast, water, salt, pepper, garlic powder, and cumin. Blend, until smooth and creamy.
2. Add 1 tbsp of water, one at a time, to thin sauce, if needed.
3. Serve chilled or warmed.

HELPFUL TIPS

Soaking the cashews overnight is recommended to ensure smooth blending, especially since this recipe has minimal liquids.This versatile sauce can be enjoyed as a dip or with whole grain crackers. Warm up the sauce for a comforting topping on baked potatoes, tacos, roasted or grilled veggies, or even Portobello mushrooms.
Recipe contains nuts and nut by-products.*

When I first created this Parmesan Cheez recipe, I never realized that it would take off like a rocket. I add it to almost everything I make, and even sneak a few small bites in while cooking.

PARMESAN CHEEZ

PREP: 10 MIN   *MAKES: 1 CUP*

INGREDIENTS

1 cup almonds

4 tbsp nutritional yeast

1 tsp garlic powder

½ tsp salt

DIRECTIONS

1. In small food processor or coffee grinder, combine all ingredients.
2. Pulse or blend until mixture forms a fine powder, resembling the texture of grated Parmesan cheese.
3. Refrigerate in airtight container for up to 3 weeks.

HELPFUL TIPS

This non-dairy Parmesan cheese is perfect for sprinkling over pasta, salads, or any dish where you want a savory, cheesy flavor without dairy. Enjoy the nutty, cheesy goodness of this homemade Parmesan Cheez.

Recipe contains nuts.*

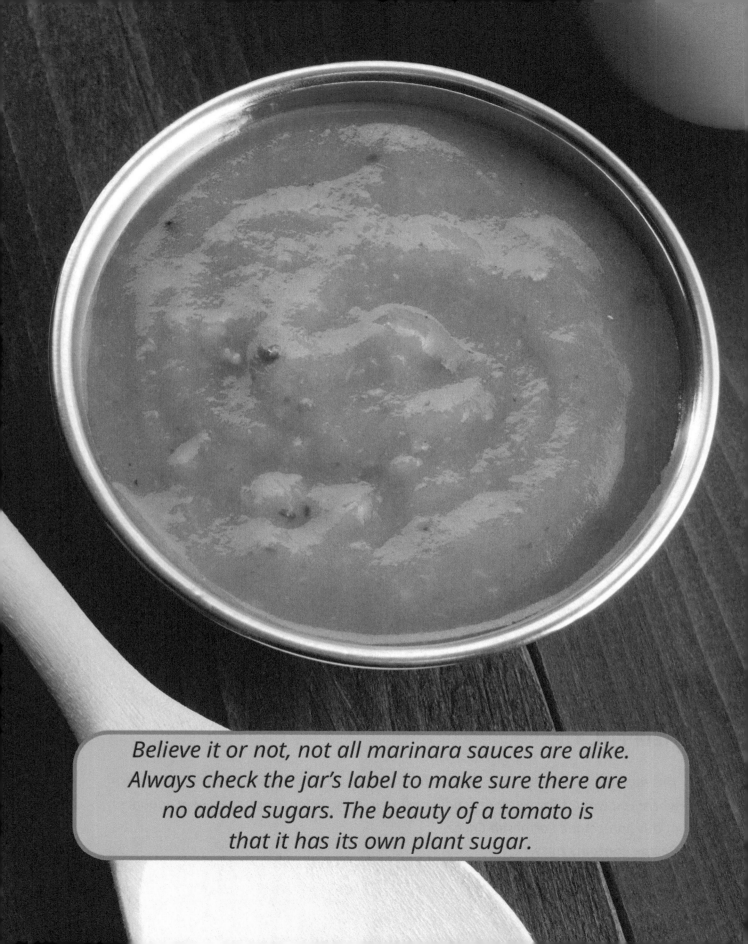

Believe it or not, not all marinara sauces are alike. Always check the jar's label to make sure there are no added sugars. The beauty of a tomato is that it has its own plant sugar.

ENHANCED MARINARA SAUCE

PREP: 10 MIN   COOK: 20 MIN   SERVES: 8

INGREDIENTS

1 jar (24 oz) marinara sauce

1 tbsp garlic powder

1 tsp onion powder

½ tsp red pepper flakes

1 tsp dried oregano

1 tsp marjoram

1 tsp dried basil

Salt and pepper, to taste

DIRECTIONS

1. Warm marinara sauce in saucepan over medium heat.
2. Stir in all remaining ingredients, and simmer over low heat, about 15-20 minutes, stirring occasionally.
3. Serve with pasta and fresh basil, or as a dipping sauce.

HELPFUL TIPS

Customize the sauce by adding plant-based meat, mushrooms, or other vegetables for additional flavor and texture. The addition of red pepper flakes provides a hint of heat, while simmering which allows the flavors to meld beautifully.

Another easy way to incorporate your leafy greens. It's a delicious routine that never gets old.

CREAMY SPINACH SAUCE

PREP: 10 MIN   *SERVES: 4*

INGREDIENTS

¾ cup raw cashews, soaked

4 cups organic baby spinach

½ cup nutritional yeast

1 lime, juiced

¾ cup water

½ tsp garlic powder

½ tsp sea salt

Pinch of black pepper

DIRECTIONS

1. Mix all ingredients in blender, until smooth and creamy.
2. Add more water for thinner sauce.
3. Serve chilled or warm.

HELPFUL TIPS

Versatile and nutritious, this sauce is ideal for drizzling over salads, brown rice, quinoa, or whole grain pasta, adding a delightful burst of flavor to your favorite dishes.
Recipe contains nut by-products.*

Kick up your vitamin C and help lower inflammation with my sassy sauce. This Romesco Sauce is absolutely loaded with antioxidants.

ROMESCO SAUCE

PREP: 10 MIN   COOK: 10 MIN   SERVES: 4

INGREDIENTS

1 jar (12 oz) roasted red pepper, drained

4 small Roma tomatoes

1 cup walnuts

¼ cup chickpeas, drained and rinsed

¼ cup fresh parsley

1 tbsp vegetable broth

3 garlic cloves

1 tbsp red wine vinegar

¼ tsp red pepper flakes or Cayenne pepper

½ tsp smoked paprika

1 tsp sweet paprika

½ tsp salt

¼ tsp black pepper

2 tbsp lemon, juiced

2 cups organic baby spinach, optional

DIRECTIONS

1. In blender, combine all ingredients, until smooth and creamy.
2. Pour into saucepan, add spinach, if using, and bring to boil over medium heat. Reduce heat, and simmer for 5 minutes, stirring occasionally.
3. Serve warm over whole grain pasta.

HELPFUL TIPS

Cold sauce makes a great dip for veggies, whole grain crusty bread, pita, or whole grain chips.
Recipe contains nuts.*

Avocado Spread
So simple to prepare. Cut. Scoop. Mash. Serve.
Imagine the possibilities.

AVOCADO SPREAD

PREP: 15 MIN   SERVES: 4

INGREDIENTS

2 avocados

1 large tomato, chopped

¼ cup onion, chopped

¼ cup bell pepper, chopped

1 tsp garlic powder

1 tsp salt

DIRECTIONS

1. In medium bowl, mash avocado, and add remaining ingredients. Mix to combine.
2. Serve chilled.

HELPFUL TIPS

Mixture can be spread on toast or wrapped in a Romaine lettuce leaf. Also can be used as a dip for fresh veggies or chips.

A different sauce for pasta. It's great to pour over steamed or roasted veggies. Dare to be different while you incorporate your greens.

PESTO SAUCE

PREP: 10 MIN   **SERVES: 4**

INGREDIENTS

2 cups organic baby spinach

2 cups kale

¼ cup raw cashews

1 tbsp dried basil

¼ cup fresh parsley

2 tbsp water

½ lime, juiced

½ tsp sea salt

¼ tsp black pepper

1 tsp garlic, minced

DIRECTIONS

1. In blender, mix all ingredients, until smooth and creamy. Add more water for thinner sauce.
2. Enjoy cold on salads or hot on your favorite pasta.

HELPFUL TIPS

If you don't like the taste of kale, substitute it with more spinach. Wonderful sauce for whole grain pasta.
Recipe contains nuts.*

Spices are not only amazing flavor additions for so many
meals, they provide another way for you to get your
antioxidants. This vibrant and versatile Mexican
Spice Blend is crafted to infuse your recipes
with authentic, bold flavors.

MEXICAN SPICE

PREP: 10 MIN

INGREDIENTS

4 tbsp chilli powder

2 tbsp ground cumin

1 tsp dried oregano

1 tbsp black pepper

2 tbsp garlic powder

2½ tbsp smoked paprika

1 tsp onion powder

¼ tsp red pepper flakes

¼ tsp Cayenne pepper

DIRECTIONS

1. In small bowl, combine all ingredients, and stir well.
2. Transfer to glass jar with lid, and store.

HELPFUL TIPS

Perfect for seasoning tacos, enchiladas, or any Mexican-inspired dish. This blend is your go-to for adding layers of flavor and a burst of spice to your meals. Use it as a dry rub, in marinades, or to kick up your favorite recipes. Try it in my Spanish Rice recipe (see page 121)

Wellness Is A State of Mind, Body And Spirit

CHAPTER 10 DESSERTS

Sweet potato for dessert? Say it ain't so!

SWEET POTATO PARFAIT

PREP: 10 MIN   COOK: 5 MIN   SERVES: 4

INGREDIENTS

1 sweet potato, cooked and cooled
2 tbsp non-dairy milk
½ banana, sliced
¼ cup non-dairy mini chocolate chips
Ground cinnamon

DIRECTIONS

1. Scoop sweet potato out of skin, place in small bowl, and stir in milk, until creamy.
2. Add banana and chocolate chips, stirring gently to combine.
3. Sprinkle with cinnamon, and serve.

HELPFUL TIPS

This is one of my favorite sweet treats. Slices of fresh banana add natural sweetness, while non-dairy mini chocolate chips provide a rich and indulgent touch, making it a versatile treat any time of day. This is a perfect breakfast for overnight guests.
Recipe contains nut by-products*

Whole grain oats, raisins, and non-dairy chocolate chips add to the sweetness of this decadent, yet healthy cookie. A dessert option that everyone can enjoy.

OATMEAL SURPRISE COOKIES

PREP: 15 MIN   COOK: 10-12 MIN   SERVES: 4

INGREDIENTS

1 cup old-fashioned oats

1 cup almond flour

½ tsp arrowroot

½ tsp ground cinnamon

¼ tsp salt

⅓ cup unsweetened applesauce

¼ cup coconut oil, melted

¼ cup pure maple syrup

1 tsp vanilla extract

½ cup raisins

½ cup non-dairy dark chocolate chips

DIRECTIONS

1. Preheat oven to 350°F.
2. In large bowl, whisk together oats, almond flour, arrowroot, cinnamon, and salt.
3. In small bowl, mix applesauce, coconut oil, maple syrup, and vanilla.
4. Pour wet ingredients into dry ingredients, and stir, until well combined.
5. Fold in raisins and chocolate chips.
6. Using a tablespoon or cookie scoop, drop dough onto baking sheet lined with parchment paper, spacing 2 inches apart.
7. Bake for 10-12 minutes, or until edges are golden brown.
8. Allow cookies to cool on baking sheet for 5 minutes, before transferring to wire rack to cool completely.

HELPFUL TIPS

Enjoy these delicious gluten-free, dairy-free, sugar-free Oatmeal Surprise Cookies with a glass of non-dairy milk. My husband Al calls this his all-time favorite cookie.
Recipe contains nut by-products.*

No added sugar in this sweet bread. Healthy fat from nuts and the natural energy from a banana can turn it into a fabulous breakfast.

BANANA NUT BREAD

PREP: 15 MIN   *COOK: 50-60 MIN*   *MAKES: 10 SLICES*

INGREDIENTS

2 cups ripe bananas (about 4 medium bananas)

⅓ cup unsweetened applesauce

2 tsp vanilla extract

2 cups oat flour, gluten-free

1 tsp baking soda

½ tsp baking powder

½ tsp salt

1 tsp ground cinnamon

½ cup walnuts or pecans, chopped

Avocado oil spray

DIRECTIONS

1. Preheat oven to 350°F.
2. In large bowl, mash bananas, until smooth, and add applesauce and vanilla. Stir, until well combined.
3. In small bowl, whisk together oat flour, baking soda, baking powder, salt, and ground cinnamon.
4. Gradually add dry ingredients to wet ingredients, stirring until just combined. Be careful not to over mix. Fold in chopped nuts.
5. Spray 9x5 inch loaf pan with avocado oil spray, pour in batter, and spread evenly.
6. Bake for 50-60 minutes, or until a toothpick inserted into center comes out clean.
7. Allow bread to cool in pan, about 10 minutes, and transfer to wire rack to cool completely before slicing.

HELPFUL TIPS

Perfect for breakfast, dessert, a gift for a friend, or hostess gift.
Recipe contains nuts*

No need for an oven with this one. The kids finish it off before you can get it in the fridge.

COOKIE DOUGH

PREP: 10 MIN   COOK: NONE   SERVES: 6

INGREDIENTS

1 can (15 oz) chickpeas, drained
and rinsed
½ cup organic peanut butter
¼ cup maple syrup
1 tsp vanilla extract
2 tbsp old-fashioned oats
Pinch of sea salt
½ cup non-dairy chocolate chips

DIRECTIONS

1. In food processor, combine all ingredients, except chocolate chips, and process until smooth.
2. Transfer to bowl, and fold in chocolate chips.
3. Spoon into small bowls, and serve.
4. Store in refrigerator for up to 4 days, or freeze and thaw. Do not bake.

HELPFUL TIPS

Enjoy this wholesome, plant-based cookie dough as a satisfying snack or a guilt-free dessert. We love our chocolate.

Recipe contains nuts, and nut by-products.*

Chocolate lovers rejoice. Not only is this decadent frozen treat delicious, it's loaded with Vitamin C from the pomegranate seeds.

POMEGRANATE BARK

PREP: 10 MIN   COOK: 5 MIN   SET/COOLING: 60 MIN   SERVES: 8

INGREDIENTS

1 package (12 oz) non-dairy
dark chocolate chips
(at least 60% cacao)
¼ cup coconut oil
¼ cup maple syrup
2 cups pomegranate seeds

DIRECTIONS

1. In saucepan over low heat, add chocolate chips and coconut oil. Stir continuously, until melted, add maple syrup, and mix well.
2. Spread evenly on baking sheet lined with parchment paper.
3. With spatula, firmly press pomegranate seeds into chocolate.
4. Place baking sheet in freezer, and allow to set for at least 1 hour.
5. Break apart, enjoy immediately, or store in freezer.

HELPFUL TIPS

Store any leftovers in the freezer to maintain the texture and freshness.
Recipe contains nut by-products.*

My family is absolutely obsessed with chocolate.
When I made this pudding recipe, they
described it as "sinfully rich".
Nobody believed that it was avocado.

AVOCADO CHOCOLATE BLISS

PREP: 10 MIN   *Refrigeration Time: 30 MIN*   *SERVES: 4*

INGREDIENTS

6 organic Medjool dates, pitted

2½ large avocados

½ cup unsweetened cocoa powder

¼ cup maple syrup

2 tsp honey

2 tsp vanilla extract

½ cup non-dairy milk

¼ tsp sea salt

DIRECTIONS

1. In high-powered blender, add all ingredients, and mix, until smooth and creamy.
2. Refrigerate, about 1 hour, to chill and firm.
3. Serve with fresh fruit or unsweetened coconut shreds.

HELPFUL TIPS

Adding different fruits, such as cherries, nuts, or even a pinch of cinnamon, can create a vast range of flavor profiles. This pudding can be stored in an airtight container in the refrigerator for up to 3 days, making it a great make-ahead dessert option. Garnish with a mint leaf.

Recipe contains nut by-products. *

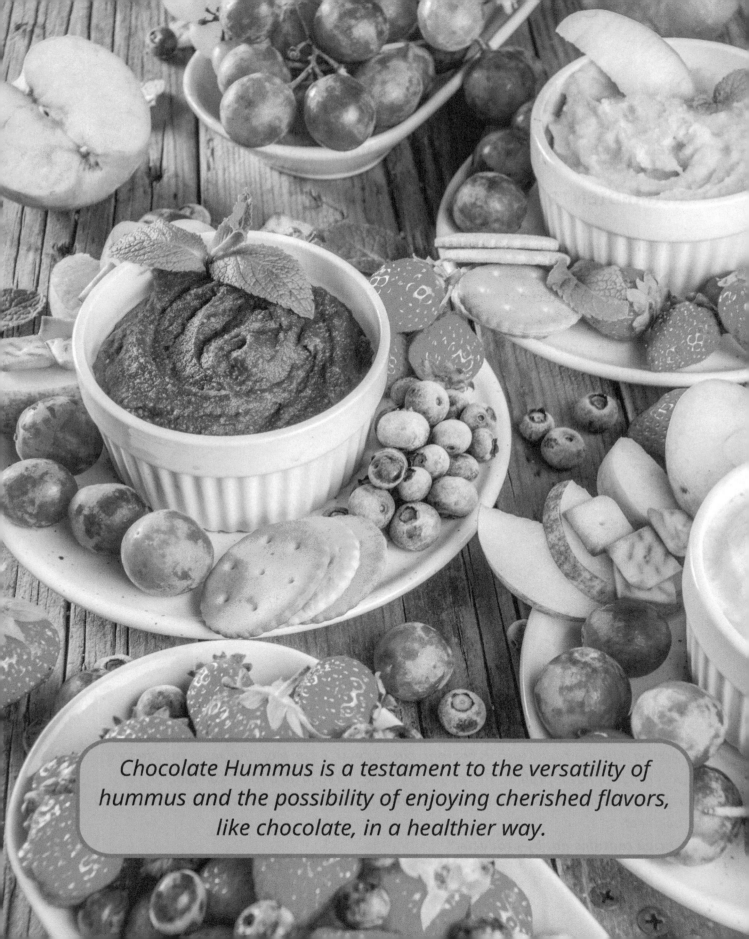

Chocolate Hummus is a testament to the versatility of hummus and the possibility of enjoying cherished flavors, like chocolate, in a healthier way.

CHOCOLATE HUMMUS

PREP: 10 MIN   REFRIGERATE: 30 MIN   SERVES: 8

INGREDIENTS

1 can (15 oz) chickpeas, drained and rinsed

¼ cup unsweetened cocoa powder

2 tbsp maple syrup

¼ cup honey

¼ cup organic almond butter

½ tsp vanilla extract

¼ tsp ground cinnamon

¼ cup non-dairy milk

DIRECTIONS

1. In high-powered blender, add all ingredients, and mix, until smooth and creamy.
2. Refrigerate for 30 minutes.
3. Transfer to decorative bowl, and serve.

HELPFUL TIPS

Serve with strawberries, apples, crackers, whole grain granola or just enjoy it by the spoonful.

Recipe contains nut by-products.*

The light touch of orange juice sets this recipe apart from the rest. Avocado Orange Pudding will be a hit with your family.

AVOCADO ORANGE PUDDING

PREP: 15 MIN   *CHILL TIME: 1 HOUR*   *SERVES: 4*

INGREDIENTS

2 large avocados

1 package (3½ oz) dark
chocolate chips, melted

3 tbsp cacao powder

2 tbsp orange juice

1 tsp vanilla extract

1 tsp ground cinnamon

¼ tsp salt

1 tbsp coconut shreds

DIRECTIONS

1. In high-powered blender, mix avocado, until smooth and creamy.
2. Add remaining ingredients, and blend well.
3. Refrigerate, about 1 hour, to chill and firm.
4. Top with coconut shreds, and serve.

HELPFUL TIPS

This dessert is smooth, luscious, and flavored with a touch of orange. For a much fancier presentation, garnish with a few Cutie Orange slices and a sprig of mint, in addition to the coconut shreds, for a refreshing treat that's indulgent, guilt-free and nice to look at.
Recipe contains nuts, and nut by-products.*

These dairy-free Pumpkin Oat Cookies are not just for Thanksgiving. Enjoy the sweetness with the benefit of no added sugar.

PUMPKIN OAT COOKIES

PREP: 15 MIN   **COOK: 12-15 MIN**   **MAKES: 18-24 COOKIES**

INGREDIENTS

1 cup pumpkin puree

½ cup unsweetened applesauce

¼ cup maple syrup

1 tsp vanilla extract

1½ cups old-fashioned oats

1 cup oat flour (Make your own: blend oats in food processor, until fine)

1 tsp ground cinnamon

½ tsp ground nutmeg

¼ tsp ground cloves

¼ tsp salt

½ cup chopped nuts

½ cup raisins or dried cranberries

DIRECTIONS

1. Preheat oven to 350°F.
2. In large bowl, combine pumpkin puree, applesauce, maple syrup, and vanilla, and mix well.
3. Add oats, oat flour, cinnamon, nutmeg, cloves, and salt. Stir, until combined.
4. Fold in nuts and raisins or cranberries.
5. Drop spoonfuls of dough onto baking sheet lined with parchment paper, spacing them 2 inches apart. If you prefer thinner cookies, flatten slightly with back of spoon.
6. Bake for 12-15 minutes, until edges are golden brown.
7. Allow to cool on baking sheet for 5 minutes before transferring to wire rack to cool completely.

HELPFUL TIPS

These cookies are great as a hostess gift, cookie exchanges, holiday parties, and get-togethers.

Recipe contains nuts and nut by products.*

Meet The Author

My name is Debbie Romano, and I am delighted to introduce myself as the author of this wonderful cookbook. As a health coach, passionate cook, and food enthusiast, I have always enjoyed spending time in the kitchen experimenting with different flavors and ingredients. Over the years, I have acquired an extensive collection of family recipes. I have experimented and adapted them to fit today's healthier lifestyle. I've had a blast over the last 12 years creating meals that actually promote good health.

My journey in Nutrition & Wellness began after my husband Al experienced a near-fatal cardiac event on July 3, 2012. During his road to recovery, I began to realize that the conventional nutrition and wellness schools of thought did not adequately address the nutritional needs and requirements of cardiac patients. The dietary suggestions they offered still seemed to allow what I believed to be far too many heart-harmful elements in the diet, so I began to conduct my own research on the subject.

Fast forward two years...I earned my Nutrition and Wellness Certification through the American Fitness Professionals & Associates and my Certification in Plant-Based Nutrition from the Campbell Center for Nutritional Studies at eCornell University. I currently operate a successful Nutrition and Wellness consulting business in Fountain Hills, which is where the idea for the cookbook was born. Many clients have asked about a cookbook of my recipes. Here it is.

The cherished recipes I've developed hold a special place in my heart, and I am thrilled to be able to share them with you through this cookbook. My hope is that these revitalized recipes will not only provide you with delicious, healthy meals, but also create new memories of cherished family moments spent together with family and friends around the table.

This cookbook offers a wide variety of recipes, ranging from simple snacks to everyday healthy meals with modern takes on classic dishes. I hope you enjoy and learn from them as much as I have!

RECIPE INDEX

RECIPE INDEX PAGE 2

Made in the USA
Monee, IL
01 October 2024

66406263R00129